Cultural Studies

Polity Short Introduction series

Published

Nicholas Abercrombie, Sociology
Michael Bury, Health and Illness
R. W. Connell, Gender
Hartley Dean, Social Policy
Stephanie Lawson, International Relations

For more information go to www.polity.co.uk/shortintroductions

Cultural Studies

Chris Rojek

polity

First published in 2007 by Polity Press

Reprinted 2007

Polity Press
65 Bridge Street
Cambridge CB2 1UR, UK

Polity Press
350 Main Street
Malden, MA 02148, USA

ISBN-13: 978-07456-3683-2
ISBN-13: 978-07456-3684-9 (pb)

A catalogue record for this book is available from the British Library.

The publishers gratefully acknowledge the cooperation of Routledge in the production of this book.

Typeset in 10 on 12 pt Sabon
by SNP Best-set Typesetter Ltd, Hong Kong
Printed and bound in Great Britain by MPG Books Ltd, Bodmin, Cornwall

The publisher has used its best endeavours to ensure that the URLs for external websites referred to in this book are correct and active at the time of going to press. However, the publisher has no responsibility for the websites and can make no guarantee that a site will remain live or that the content is or will remain appropriate.

For further information on Polity, visit our website: www.polity.co.uk

For George and Sue Ritzer, benign hosts of the 'McDonald's House' in Montgomery County, martini makers nonpareil, and a couple manifesting great and continuing warmth, kindness and good sense . . . (Although watch those terms in the contract next time George!)

Contents

Culture Counts

Every human culture produces general narratives, some based upon common experience, others upon the selective experience of an elite or ruling class, expressed as binding and sometimes sacred truths, designed to achieve solidarity and a shared sense of the past. For every human society consists of individuals and groups positioned in relations of unequal access to scarce economic, political, social and cultural resources. Because of this, those who acquire dominance have developed alliances and traditions designed to legitimate rule and, upon this basis, have participated in threading together a web of common rights, justice, truth, ideals, myths and traditions to protect and advance their interests. Like all groups they are unable to fully control the consequences of their actions, even though they typically behave in public as if the opposite is the case. Strategies and designs that have been planned to enhance their position often have unintended consequences that return to haunt them in the course of time.

Since dominant groups are in relations of privilege over other groups, it follows that their position is directly and indirectly subject to challenge and contest. Groups that challenge authority develop their own cultures of resistance and opposition. These are modified through interplay with dominant groups. Through this perpetual interchange and elaboration culture grows.

The inevitable consequence of these cultural, social, economic and political struggles is the assignment of credence to the necessarily partial views of the powerful in respect of the shared past and the common interest. Why? Sir John Harrington's (1561–1612) oft-quoted bon mot deserves repeating here:

> Treason doth never prosper, what's the reason?
> For if it prosper, none dare call it treason.

In other words, the acquisition of cultural authority carries with it the capacity to re-write history and redefine the nature of the present. But cultural authority is seldom an open and shut case. Cultural interchange produces unforeseen results and domination means that some groups are disempowered and marginalized. However, domination and disempowerment are never absolute. Even the Muslim prisoners held by the Americans at the Abu Ghraib camp, on what many expert international lawyers regard to be dubious legal grounds, can protest and challenge authority. One of the heartening lessons to be learned from doing Cultural Studies is that dominant groups are not all-powerful. They are caught up in the unintended, unanticipated consequences of intended cultural design like everyone else. Of course, their capacity to influence these consequences is typically greater than that of the average person or group. Nonetheless, they are subject to limitations and constraints especially if their behaviour incites public censure or provokes condemnation.

The local and the global

In emphasizing the global reach of contemporary culture it is important to not get carried away. Culture is always local as well as global. National and global culture often rub against the conditions of life that people experience, as it were, 'on the ground', in their own local spaces and traditions. Resistance and opposition are the accessories of cultural authority, for groups are always positioned differently in relation to scarce resources and therefore develop various, contrasting traditions of rights, justice and truth. For this reason they build many types of cultural solidarity and conflicting ways of reading the past, and engage in frictional ways of interpreting the world.

When it was made public that three of the suicide bombers who attacked London in 2005 were *British* and the fourth was Anglo-Jamaican, it triggered a fusillade of national and international debate. Why would British Muslims want to murder and maim their own countrymen? The answer, of course, is that the four men identified with a form of radical Islam that made their nationality, where they lived, their neighbours and their fellow workers, beside the point. The Arab satellite broadcasting company Al Jazeera TV aired a video 'suicide note' by the alleged ringleader of the bombers, Mohammad Sadique Khan. Speaking in a strong Yorkshire accent, the 30-year-old, former teaching assistant, proactively justified the London bombs by referring to unparticularized 'crimes against humanity' perpetrated by Western governments in the Arab region and the huge wealth of the West in comparison with the relative poverty of the developing world. In attacking Londoners, Khan and his fellow suicide bombers saw themselves as striking a blow against Anglo-American imperialism in Iraq and Palestine. Their self-image was of righteous religious warriors avenging the oppressed and marginalized thousands of miles away in the Arabian subcontinent. Yet the constituency of Islamic people that supported the London suicide bombs is dubious. Islamic leaders in Britain and other countries quoted from passages in the Koran to condemn the bombers as criminals rather than religious warriors.

The number of British Muslims who support the indiscriminate killing of fellow civilians as a legitimate response to Anglo-American involvement in the post-Saddam reconstruction of Iraq is infinitesimal. Why then did Khan and his conspirators believe they were acting for either a larger body of opinion or a greater good, which they hoped to render manifest by dint of the explosives they triggered on three London underground trains and a bus? What makes individuals and groups raised and nurtured by a host national culture define themselves in diametric opposition to the values of that culture so that they are prepared to obliterate themselves and others who have done no wrong against them and who may, for all they know, share the outlook that they hold and aim to promulgate?

Similar questions were raised earlier in the USA in the trials of the Oklahoma City bombers Timothy McVeigh and Terry Nichols and the Unabomber, Ted Kacynski. McVeigh had served with the American military in the Gulf War; Kacynski was a former assistant Professor of Mathematics at the University of California at Berkeley. Both saw themselves as American patriots and rejected the US government for, in their view, having hoodwinked and betrayed the people. They seized on the American doctrines of individualism and freedom of conscience to justify killing and injuring fellow citizens. In McVeigh's case, the main motivation was state spin, and the repression of the right to free speech for right-wing groups. Kacynski operated with a more complex set of motivations set out in his notorious 35,000-word *Unabomber Manifesto* published in 1995 in the *New York Times* and the *Washington Post*. Here, in measured and rather compelling tones that would have not disgraced many legitimate, established critics of contemporary culture, Kacynski set out a condemnation of industrial civilization that centres upon its role in destroying the environment, fine-tuning conformity, spreading misinformation, expanding surveillance powers, producing ubiquitous sex and violence on television and assigning too much autonomy to multinational corporations.

Media genre and cultural representation

Our knowledge of these figures and the events associated with them is transmitted to us through the media. The media isn't just an impartial relayer of news and information. It is a complex multi-corporate/state network that codes and packages data for public consumption. Different media organizations such as the BBC, CNN, Fox News, Al Jazeera TV, ABC, CBS, *The Guardian*, the *New York Times*, *Le Monde*, the *Toronto Globe & Mail*, the *Los Angeles Times*, the *London Evening Standard*, the *New York Post* and *The Australian* have distinctive styles of reporting and addressing audiences. Media genre is not just a question of presentational style, it also includes questions of relevance, judgements about the national and international significance of items and the cultural and political agenda that informs these processes of selection. These reflect not only national characteristics but also distinctive cultural traditions of journalism and broadcasting. To this extent, the news, just like the companies that package and code it for us, is *branded*.

Among the best rationales for doing Cultural Studies is that it shows why the human world is very often not what it seems to be and offers a disciplined way of exposing how communication and representation serve the interests behind power and manipulation. The common rights, traditions and truths at our disposal often turn out to be illusions disguising powerful social interests and complex political devices designed to achieve compliance. By critically examining them, we discover an intricately staged version of our pooled traditions of truth and justice, and what frequently turns out to be a mythical version of our shared past.

The metaphor of *staging* suggests that there is someone or something behind the deception who wilfully engages in the craft of concealment and fabrication. To be sure, there can be no doubt that the powerful engage in systematic distortion to disguise the full range of their might and the inner nature of their social, political and economic interests. It would be rash and perverse to discount the formidable nature of their power. Yet if it is right to describe them as puppeteers, history has a habit of tying them up in their own strings. The interplay of culture creates unplanned outcomes that condition the options for intentional action for all.

Myth has certainly been used by the mighty to manipulate and control ordinary people. But myths have also been developed by ordinary people to give meaning to complex and bewildering events.

The 9/11 atrocity was so shocking and incompatible with the basic tenets of Islam that some Muslims responded with the submission that the CIA had concocted the attacks to throw Islam into disarray. The devastating tsunami that killed hundreds of thousands in South East Asia in December 2004 was explained by some conservatives as the punishment of God for human waywardness. Myths have cultural origins and they are typically elaborated in culture wars.

There are many ways in which this can be investigated in Cultural Studies. We don't need to start with abstract concepts like 'ideology', 'hegemony' or 'interpellation' to describe how cultural authority is imposed; or 'hybridity', 'encoding' or 'decoding' to investigate how cultural authority is contested. As we will see later, these concepts have their place in the subject. But the root and branch of culture is about how you and others around you are organized as persons. It is about why one person believes that free university education is good, and another insists that students must pay their way; or why Muslims generally tolerate arranged marriages, while Westerners typically deplore them. Culture is about brass tacks. It influences our choice of friends, sexual partners, diet, jobs, leisure activities and many other issues besides. It explains much about how we live and how we die. Because we experience culture as individuals it is easy to imagine that our private world is unique. But culture is public. It is the system of representation through which we render ourselves unto ourselves and others, as 'individuals', 'unique persons' and 'social agents'. By studying it we gain knowledge of how even the most private experience is culturally enmeshed.

The meaning of culture

The term 'culture' derives from the Latin *cultura*. The original meaning was agricultural, referring to the practice of tilling the soil, growing crops and raising animals. Understandably, Cultural Studies has paid scant attention to this obsolete meaning. Instead, it proceeds on the basis that the term 'culture' today carries dual *social* meanings having to do with urban-industrial forms of knowledge and power. Knowledge here is understood as both concrete ideas about the meaning of culture and technical ideas about how to communicate meanings to best effect. Power refers to the unequal distribution of economic, cultural and political resources in society, and the changing balance of influence and force attached to this state of affairs. Cultural Studies insists upon conceptualizing culture as the intersection of force and resistance. There are many shared ingredients of popular reality. But much of it is *struggled* over, contested and opposed.

The first of the twin meanings in common currency today is *evaluative*. It refers to culture as the cultivation of mind, taste, manners, artistic accomplishments and the scientific and intellectual attainments of a particular people. This meaning is *hierarchical* since it portrays culture as the summit of achievement among a body of people. Of course, culture is something that a social stratum, typically conceptualized as an elite, or ruling class possesses. The non-elite, usually identified as the mass or 'the people', are acknowledged to create cultures of their own. But they are generally assumed to be inferior, or secondary.

The second meaning is *narrative*. It refers to the bundle of beliefs, myths, customs, practices, quirks and the general way of life that is characteristic of a specific population. This is a descriptive approach to culture that recounts the ordinary features of life that predominate among a people. Anthropologists, historians and sociologists have had the lion's share in elaborating our understanding of the narrative content and patterns of culture. But the contribution of Cultural Studies is increasingly significant, especially through the use of how representation frames popular reality and the multiple realities of culture revealed through ethnography and other forms of qualitative research.

Expressed concisely, Cultural Studies has spent much of its history dismantling the first meaning of culture while simultaneously elucidating the role of knowledge and power in influencing the second. This sounds like a dry business. Yet, ironically, the birth of Cultural Studies was attended by considerable notoriety. Why was this? Above all else, treating popular culture seriously impacted against the condescension of elite groups, for the most rarefied of whom, the masses were held to be more or less incapable of generating worthwhile cultural content or form. To declare value in forms of resistance in schooling, to study comics and cartoon characters as signs of knowledge and power, or to treat media panics over mugging as a barometrical reading of the crisis in the state was akin to hurling a mixture of salt and pepper in the face of the establishment. Even those in the turreted elite of a more liberal ilk bridled at the application of the term 'culture' to describe classroom troublemakers, adolescent female consumers of comics and, above all, convicted young criminals. From their point of view these elements were the antithesis of culture, because they posed a threat to the peace of society. What was needed for them was not understanding or tolerance but a hard, no-nonsense policy consisting of clear rules of behaviour and zero tolerance.

Notions of 'peace' and 'common sense' were of course viewed through elite spectacles, but they were assumed to be universal and self-evident. In arguing that elite values distorted and manipulated culture, Cultural Studies was held in some quarters to be an activity bordering on subversion.

But Cultural Studies actually went further than this. It submitted that the content and form of culture is moulded by knowledge and power and is the means not only of controlling and manipulating people, but also for resisting inequality and domination. By relating questions of culture to matters of political control and social leadership, Cultural Studies therefore questioned the prevailing balance of power in society. More particularly, the authority of elite groups and the relevance of their characteristic knowledge and power were taken to task. The practice of Cultural Studies made every received cultural tradition, set of assumptions and official explanation of social and cultural reality up for grabs. Nothing could be treated as sacred or beyond discussion any more. Indeed, one of the most powerful consequences of Cultural Studies is that this emphasis upon demystification and deconstruction made *everything* a legitimate subject for study. Traditional ideas that some cultural issues were too 'trivial' to study were redefined by students of Cultural Studies as a cause célèbre.

The culture of 'friendly fire'

Consider the case of Corporal Patrick D. Tillman, a member of the US Army Rangers, who at 27 was killed in an Afghan ravine in April 2004 (see figure 1.1). After his death, Patrick was celebrated in the media as an all-American hero. He enlisted following the 9/11 attacks, after turning his back on a lucrative career as a defensive back in the American National Football League. He was motivated by the example of his grandfather who served at Pearl Harbor, and a conviction that his country was imperilled by foreign foes. But on many fronts, the truth was more complicated.

Initially his death was described as the result of a 'fire-fight'. It was not until the publication of the official inquiry, a year later, that the full facts emerged. Tillman had been killed by 'friendly fire' in an act of 'gross negligence', in the words of a US army investigator. He was the victim of a collapse in 'situational awareness' that resulted in two groups of

Fig. 1.1.   Patrick Tillman © AP/EMPICS

American soldiers mistaking one another for the enemy, and discharging their weapons against each other.

Tillman is an interesting modern American hero. An atheist, an anti-war activist and an ally of the prominent left-wing critic Noam Chomsky – he was scheduled to meet Chomsky on his return from Afghanistan – he nonetheless volunteered to go to war in a cause about which he entertained grave doubts. Perhaps his involvement in the world of American sports exploited and developed a sort of knee-jerk nationalism in his personality. Tillman would not be the first or last intelligent young critic of American foreign policy to decide that in the end he was for his country, right or wrong.

For students of Cultural Studies a number of fascinating questions are suggested by this incident. What culture of masculinity created Patrick Tillman? How was his close identification with the culture of national interests engineered? In what ways did he handle his reservations about the war during his time of service? How are 'allies' and 'enemies' culturally coded and recognized? What makes 'situational awareness' collapse? Why did military officials seek to disguise the manner of his death? What has the anti-war movement done to make an issue of the circumstances of his death?

These questions belong to the sphere of cultural politics, and they are legitimate, indeed one might say, *necessary* topics for Cultural Studies. Why necessary? Because they reveal the public calculus behind 'private' choices, the complex intended and unintended forces that present a truncated view of the past as binding and point to the motivations of the cultural interests who try to tailor history to fit their own cloth. By investigating these topics we have the chance of becoming better acquainted with how meaning is presented and resisted in common culture. In a word, we stand the chance of becoming *better* citizens.

Cultural Studies is frontally concerned with political issues. This is inevitable because individuals and groups are positioned in a set of unequal relationships with respect to scarce economic, social, cultural and political resources. But there is more to the subject than a political focus.

2

Doing Cultural Studies

I submit that there are four interrelated components of Cultural Studies, having to do with the *observation* of culture (genre), the *manufacture* of culture (production), the *exchange* of culture (consumption) and the *contestation* of culture (cultural politics). Let us examine them in more detail.

1 *Genre*, or the patterning of cultural form and content. What types of culture do people identify with recognition and belonging? How does Goth culture represent itself? What devices do women's magazines use to attract readers? What are the characteristics of House and Techno culture? How does *American Pop Idol* differ from its British equivalent? In what ways do cultures of cuisine signify power and difference? What do motor racing enthusiasts have in common? How do Chinese tourist websites represent backpacker experience? How does Afro beat hip hop differ from Afropean basement and pop? What are the main identifying features of Eminem's fan base? What are the characteristics of the gun lobby in America? Questions of genre address the characteristics of cultural form and content. They enable us to compare and contrast cultural formations and construct cartographies of cultural difference.

2 *Production* has to do with the creation of cultural meaning and the interests behind the presentation of cultural form and content. Why are people like Patrick Tillman prepared to die for their country? In what ways do multinationals apply branding to generate desire in consumer culture? In what ways do the media fan popular consciousness of news and culture? What cultural meanings are Vodafone, Adidas, Pepsi, Brylcreem, Police Sunglasses and Rage Computer and Video Games trying

to connect with consumers by employing David Beckham to endorse their products? How has Apple Mac sought to use cultural references to enlarge iPod market share? How do Manchester United or the Chicago Bears recruit and unite fans? How does the state's control of licensing influence cultural behaviour? How do deviant subcultures emerge and protect their privacy? The topic of production addresses the blueprint and application of cultural meaning. It examines the means and ends involved in traditions and projects of cultural reproduction.

3 *Consumption* refers to the various processes of how cultural meanings are assimilated, by consumers. How are cultural texts exchanged? What factors influence the assimilation of cultural meaning? What are the cultural barriers that have to date prevented the e-book from taking off in consumer culture? How is cultural form and content developed to signify difference and opposition? What are the various cultural meanings of sunglasses? How does tourist experience of Jamaica coincide with and differ from the representations of travel brochures? What are the cultural meanings of *Beavis and Butthead* or *The Osbournes* or *The Simpsons*? How do audiences subvert cultures of authority? Questions of reception focus upon the response of consumers to cultural commodities and meanings. They concentrate on the interface between cultural production and exchange. They require us to consider the field of culture, including the traditions and orientations that consumers bring to the exchange process.

4 *CulPol* (Cultural politics) refers to how meaning is presented, resisted and opposed through the process of cultural exchange. CulPol confronts issues of values, difference, knowledge and power. How is cultural form and content developed to signify difference and opposition? In what ways can brand culture be resisted? What should the balance between access and excellence be in higher education? Why do some human groups have greater influence over the media than others? Upon what basis in 2005 did Larry Summers, the President of Harvard University, claim that women possess a lower aptitude for engineering and the natural sciences than men? What doctrinal objections did the managers of Westminster Abbey have in mind in 2005 to refuse £100,000 for filming the *Da Vinci Code* in the Abbey precincts? Why do many traditional Americans oppose stem cell research? How has the anti-smoking movement succeeded in decreasing levels of tolerance in the West to smoking in public? In what ways do school subcultures challenge the cultural order imposed by teachers? Cultural politics investigates how we are differently situated in relation to scarce economic, social, political and cultural resources and the struggles and alliances that arise from this.

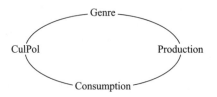

Fig. 2.1. The sphere of Cultural Studies

It raises issues of cultural authority, distributive justice and empowerment.

Cultural Studies then might be defined as the exploration of interrelationships between genre, production, consumption and cultural politics (see figure 2.1).

Precisely because staged versions of history and the truth are intricately constructed, revealing the forces that empower them is often tricky. One good way of approaching these questions is by means of comparative and historical analysis. Why? Two natural fallacies that people often make in ordinary life are that their experience is universal and that fundamental things have always been the same. By comparing cultural, political and economic conditions in other societies with those of our own (comparative analysis), and examining how people thought and acted in other times (historical analysis), we stand the chance of developing a perspective on what is common and what is unique. A comparative-historical approach is one of the surest ways of avoiding the errors of assuming that what is true of the locality which we inhabit is true everywhere and that the fundamentals of life have always been the same irrespective of society, culture and history. Moreover, it does not require great technical expertise or ability to apply. Everyone can imagine and readily research how conditions of culture vary between countries and different historical times.

Doing Cultural Studies 1: the case of Reality TV

Although a comparative and historical perspective is a prerequisite, there are several ways of doing Cultural Studies. The discipline is not like legal studies, medicine or engineering in which a well-established tradition of facts and positions must be interrogated, internalized and applied. On the contrary, at the heart of Cultural Studies is the notion that facts are not meaningful except in relation to other meanings. In other words, a fact is not a thing but a *representation*. Its meaning derives from the position it occupies in a field of communication. Moreover, these fields are not inert. They change, often in rapid and unexpected ways. This complicates the task of building a fixed, universal curriculum in Cultural Studies.

Compared with traditional culture, modern culture is super-dynamic. Genres come and go with tremendous speed. Take the example of Reality TV. A decade ago Reality TV was unknown. Today programmes like *Big Brother*, *Survivor*, *The Osbournes* and *Celebrity Chef* have developed international followings. In the case of Ozzy Osbourne or a chef such as Gordon Ramsay, their existing fame is magnified and repositioned. More interestingly, people plucked from the rank-and-file are elevated, however temporarily, into stardom. The suspension of the hierarchy between celebrity ascendance and the audience exposes questions about the nature of fame and the 'docility' of consumers. Reality TV operates by staging improbable combinations of people in confined situations and recording the results. What happens when you invite someone to marry a millionaire on live TV? How do you respond as an adopted child when you are faced by a bunch of men you have never met before, one of whom is purported to be your natural father? What happens when you mix an aggressive personality with passive ones in a house share? Such television is enormously attractive to TV broadcasting companies because it is cheap to produce yet has the capacity to generate mass audiences in the ratings wars.

Most of us think that Reality TV is an entirely new genre. A comparative and historical approach corrects this misconception. An interest in using television to illuminate the rules of everyday life and educate the public has been a long-standing feature of public broadcasting. In the 1960s, *Candid Camera* aired in the USA (fronted by Allen Funt) and a cover version appeared in Britain (with Bob Monkhouse as presenter and Jonathan Routh as lead prankster). The format was a Reality TV version of everyday life disrupted by planned events organized by the producers of the programmes. Funt and Routh inserted themselves into routine life situations with the intention of overturning them. By breaking down the conventions of behaviour in settings like shops, bus queues or highway traffic, the presenters engineered exchanges in which the human condition was humorously, and often ironically, addressed. In the 1970s, a *cinéma vérité* approach evolved in *An American Family* (directed by Craig Gilbert, 1973) and the British version, *The Family* (directed by Paul Watson, 1974). These programmes were produced as fly-on-the-wall documentaries about life in a 'typical' family, filmed over several months, with disclosures edited to tell a story, often with a clear moral message attached to each broadcast episode.

Today satellite broadcasting allows for a more varied and intense diet of Reality TV because it permits sustained, live, unedited broadcasting. This changes how we position ourselves in relation to broadcast data. Two aspects to this point must be differentiated.

Firstly, because satellite transmission theoretically permits continuous live broadcasts, it alters the rules of the genre of Reality TV. Shows like *An American Family* and *The Family* were edited and produced as documentaries designed to have a *pedagogic* effect. By living with the Wilkins family in the BBC's series *The Family*, viewers were invited to make practical, moral and strategic judgements about the behaviour displayed on-screen and, by implication, to apply this to their own lives.

Conversely, today's Reality TV operates in what John Corner (2002) argues is a *post-documentary* genre. That is, Reality TV presents 'a slice of life' and is non-judgemental. Of course, the people who are being filmed make judgements about each other's behaviour. So do the audience watching at home. But these judgements are not part of the planned production values of the programme. Yet Reality TV is not like 'real' life. This applies both on-screen and for the consumer. The players may grow accustomed to the cameras but they are also aware of inhabiting a goldfish bowl watched by millions; and the audience is conscious that players are projecting behavioural traits and opinions to affect the voting powers of the TV audience. The fact that judgements about the difference between reality and illusion are constantly made in shows like *Big Brother* and *I'm A Celebrity Get Me Out Of Here* raises the question of the nature of Reality TV as a cultural genre. This brings me to my second point.

To propose that Sharon Osbourne in *The Osbournes* or Johnny Rotten and Peter Andre in *I'm A Celebrity . . . Get Me Out Of Here*, Abi Titmuss in *Celebrity Love Island*, or, for that matter, a participant in *Big Brother* are acting 'normally' or 'naturally' on-screen is central to the conventions of the broadcast, but a moment's thought renders it implausible. However 'comfortable' they may feel in front of the camera, and regardless of the length of time that they are followed by its lens, they are still conscious of performing 'on-screen' in order to achieve an effect in the viewers watching at home. This dictates the pattern of behaviour that viewers see. A greeting between two people on a city street carries a different 'note' than a meeting between two who know that they are being filmed for global television. If this is the case, it raises issues about the kind of 'reality' that Reality TV is actually transmitting. Nick Couldry's (2003, 2004) suggestion that Reality TV exploits and develops *rituals* of performance is surely valid. Logically, it must be right to maintain that participants relate to the programme as a staged event. Because behaviour is always conditioned by the knowledge that it is enacted before a TV audience, its register and quality is different from everyday life. It is performance in a different *key*. This is why Couldry's use of the term 'ritual' to describe the performance of participants and the reactions of the audience is apposite. Rather than reflecting reality, Reality TV reflects how rituals of behaviour designed to convey reality are *performed* for *TV transmission* and *consumed* in consumer culture – especially when an interactive, voting element is involved as is the case with *Big Brother* and *I'm A Celebrity . . . Get Me Out Of Here.*

What makes us want to watch others performing the rituals that we practise in everyday life? Why should 'slice of life' shows appeal to us? These are matters for empirical research. Even so, there is no harm in doing a little speculating.

Proposition 1: *Reality TV calls upon the audience to decode a cultural genre by comparing it with 'real life'*

Saturation in the media has schooled audiences in the protocol and cultural repertoire of media interaction and created a sort of eternal friction in culture between media representation and 'real' experience. As consumers of images and representations we are perpetually engaged in trying to separate what is true from what is false, what is real and what is an illusion. Staging 'a slice of real life' on the TV screen engages us, because it invites us to decode the rituals of TV performance and strive to separate them from ordinary or everyday emotions and responses. The latter, of course, are themselves influenced by media protocols and scripts. So a sort of double-coding process is intuitively recognized to be at work here: 'real life' is coded by the characteristics of the media genre, and 'television culture' is read as a coded medium of representation that is separate from 'real life'. Drawing the line between these two sets of frictions is what Reality TV demands of the audience. Programmes are engrossing because they demand the audience to work out what is being 'played out' for the screen and make judgements about what is truly driving individual behaviour.

If all of life is a performance, there is an obvious interest in watching how others perform with one another on screen to acquire votes. The audience is invited to be both voyeur and judge. The emphasis on audience attraction is upon both *empathizing with and reading cultural genre* (the characteristics of performance and how performance is presented in order to acquire votes). *Big Brother* is a puzzle consisting of cosmetic emotions, staged responses, calculated initiatives and uncontrollable passions. But that is the same puzzle that the audience is embroiled in as the condition of real life. Watching how it unfolds on the screen, and trying to separate it from the rituals of presentation in TV culture, is what hooks the audience and wins ratings wars.

Proposition 2: *Reality TV is a spectacular version of the power relations the audience experiences in everyday life*

Following Foucault (1977, 1979), one might propose that the many positions/stances/fronts that we *present* in everyday life reflect how we are *positioned* in relation to scarce cultural, political, economic and social resources. Positioning implies governmentality. Couldry (2004) makes a perceptive point when he argues that part of the appeal of watching contestants under the microscope in shows like *Big Brother* is that the audience is accustomed in everyday life to conducting themselves under the spotlight of surveillance. It is as if the mice have been magically transformed into rulers with life and death voting powers, watching the spectacle of others as they struggle to impress, goad, solicit sympathy and in other ways connect with the invisible audience in TV-land. There is a voyeuristic aspect at work here, but it doesn't lie principally in empathizing with or reading cultural genre. Rather it rests in recognizing the power games played out on-screen as representations of the same conflicts and frictions that we encounter in ordinary life.

Schooling and the workplace have developed their own technologies of monitoring behaviour. Our emotions, especially our aggressive and sexual instincts, can only be displayed and expressed in controlled, sequestered settings. We live in a society of surveillance and governance. The television programme assumes a literal 'Big Brother' who sets the contestants tasks, monitors them and always knows more about the 'reality' than the screen situation implies. And in the subtle type of governance developed in Western democracy, in which patterning is conventionally mistaken for freedom, perhaps shows like *Big Brother*, *Pop Idol* and *I'm A Celebrity . . . Get Me Out Of Here* are popular because they dramatize the human condition. They provide metaphors for the absurd entanglements, delightful glimpses of 'liberty' and personality/organizational clashes that we experience in our everyday lives as 'governed individuals' existing under the spotlight of surveillance. As such, they keep us in our seats, watching the human comedy, pathos (of rejection) and triumph unfold.

Proposition 3: *Reality TV is pure escapism, allowing us to forget our own cares and worries by observing the antics of others as they seek to gain our attention and sympathy*

Drawing on a different tradition that portrays modern life as a series of opportunities and snares, this proposition invites us to regard Reality TV as an expression of the carnivalesque in the midst of 'McDonaldized' society. The concept of McDonaldization was coined by the American sociologist George Ritzer (1992). It means the application and colonization of principles of predictability, calculation, control and efficiency into everyday life. The advantages are that the conditions of life are experienced as more uniform, and the practice of dealing with them are rendered more convenient since, within limits, everyone knows what to expect. The disadvantages are that the standardization of behaviour is experienced as a levelling down or flattening of experience. A culture of the routine may be safe and reliable, but for many it is also boring and unchallenging.

Mikhail Bakhtin (1968) suggested a way in which human societies combat tendencies of standardization, and the general levelling of experience: periodically, they stand this order on its head. He examined Carnival as a culture of escape, resistance and tension release. His benchmark was the Medieval Carnival, with its knowing and parodic annual inversion of the routine, efficiency, predictability, calculation and control of its day.

Carnival plucks 'play' from the periphery of everyday life and places it into the centre. This manoeuvre allows people to let off steam. In Carnival pent-up emotions are released and Play is the lord of all he surveys. Might Reality TV perform a carnivalesque function of controlled tension release? By watching the strutting postures, aggressive exchanges, sexual games and competitive rivalries of the contestants, might we possess an interface which helps us to cope with our own frustrations more effectively? In Bakhtin's work, the Carnival has a therapeutic effect in off-loading the repressed tensions that accumulate in cultures in which groups and individuals are unequally situated in relation to scarce resources. Proposition 3 suggests that the same line of reasoning might be followed in examining why Reality TV has become so popular.

Doing Cultural Studies 2: The internet

Rapid change in culture is especially evident in relation to technology. Although internet technology was pioneered and applied by the military in the late 1960s, the internet as a mass phenomenon was unknown ten years ago. The stock market debut of Netscape.com occurred in 1995 and ushered in the dot.com boom (and bust) and renewed boom. Today the web is everywhere in the developed industrial societies and economic and technological urgency is focused upon developing ever faster means of net communication. The media regulator Ofcom reported in 2005 that 8 million people in the UK are connected to broadband. A variety of cultural forms such as blogging sites, chat rooms, bulletin boards, web cameras, internet telephony, discussion forums and other web and text rings have emerged from the web. The growth of this phenomenon is remarkable. For example, the tracking site Technorati reported that a new blog is created every second in the web community (*The Guardian* 7.10.05).

The development of search engines, such as Google, Yahoo and MSN, has transformed how we consume news, weather reports and communicate data. Web companies such as Amazon, eBay and Yahoo revolutionized the way in which millions buy books, electronic goods, automobiles, insurance policies and mortgages, and trade stocks and shares. The dynamics of intimate relations have been partly redefined by the web. Web-dating is one of the fastest growing trends on the internet and 'Personals' is arguably the most popular of all internet genres. Couples meet and flirt on the net, exchange photographs and make dates with an ease, flexibility and anonymity that was unimaginable a decade ago. File-sharing companies like Napster, Kazaa, Morpheus and Grockster introduced the practice of the free downloading of recorded music and film and raised massive new dilemmas about copyright over intellectual property and issues of legal access. More generally, the net has eroded the place of the shop in retail experience. The probability is that it will eventually make many levels of retailing obsolete for it cuts out the middleman, with all of the cost savings and price reductions that potentially this entails.

Similarly, at the levels of culture and politics, the development of the internet as a mass phenomenon expanded the public sphere to a scale that is unprecedented in human history. It vastly magnified the volume of knowledge and information available to the billion or so regular web surfers. Almost overnight, unlimited data on health, the law, civil rights, sex education, sport, geography, history, the arts and science became widely available. This changed the ways in which knowledge is researched and communicated. Social movements concerned with the care of the environment, the infringement of human rights, animal rights, the moral issues raised by genetic engineering, ethnic and religious difference had access to a new resource of data gathering and exchange that was effectively impossible to monitor or control. As such, the internet might be said to represent a major development in the enlargement of civil society, supplying citizens with a vast, renewable resource of data that potentially revolutionizes their capacity to participate in society, culture, politics and the economy.

The Red Guard, the panopticon and the web

Outwardly the development of the internet strengthens democracy, for it poses many problems for governments which seek to dominate through central control of the police, the military, the economy and the media. The liberalization of economy, culture and society in China since the mid-1990s coincided with the expansion of the web. This is no accident. The Chinese Communist Party leader Mao Zedong governed Chinese Communism in the 1930s with a rod of iron based on strict Bolshevik principles of inflexible central control. This assumed the priority of the Party in all aspects of everyday life, with Mao, of course, holding the banker's position as the ultimate arbiter between right and wrong. The cult of leadership is now known to have produced many human rights violations. For example, the notorious Cultural Revolution between 1965 and 1975 sprang from Mao's fear that the Chinese road to communism was threatened by creeping Westernization and the sclerosis of old, wasteful traditions. The Cultural Revolution demanded a return to fundamental Communist Party principles. It demanded an end to pre-Communist traditions, no deviation and no liberalization. Western fashion, literature and political ideas that conflicted with the communist state, films and music, even Western haircuts, were banished. Old traditions were denounced and their supporters attacked and chastised. The youth movement of the Red Guard was encouraged to disseminate the values of the Cultural Revolution by implanting them in their communities and pitilessly hunting down and penalizing dissenters. The result was hugely increased levels of surveillance, a heightened general sense of insecurity in ordinary life, and a wave of state-sponsored killings. Every neighbour, indeed every child, was turned into a potential informer. The Red Guard did not act alone. Workers were urged to toil for their allotted eight hours a day and then devote part of their leisure to advancing the revolution by monitoring others and reporting dissent. At the heart of the whole process was the revival of the cult of Mao, who was celebrated as a heroic and infallible leader. His road to communism was celebrated as not only inevitable, but inherently noble. All criticism was treated as proof of bad faith, deviance, Western corruption or mental illness.

From today's vantage point, the Chinese Cultural Revolution seems transparently authoritarian and punitive. It entailed colossal human rights abuses. Thousands of suspects were tortured and executed. Countless more lost their jobs or were demoted. It now seems obvious that cruelty, zealotry and the crude desire for total control by the Maoist faction in the Communist Party was the real engine driving the process. Doubtless some recruits to the Red Guard, workers and party officials exploited the revolution as an opportunity for personal advancement. But the majority were true believers, inspired by the utopian impulse to advance the values of equality and freedom that communism was meant to deliver to all who voluntarily submitted to its rule. For them, the Cultural Revolution had nothing to do with political domination or cultural authoritarianism. On the contrary, it was the necessary cultural response required by the threats to the communist road identified by Chairman Mao.

Michel Foucault (1977) used the *panopticon* as a metaphor for the disciplined society in the nineteenth century. The panoptican is a central observation tower, developed in blueprints of the ideal Victorian prison, from which prison officials are able to monitor the behaviour of inmates round the clock. Foucault argued that the panopticon is a metaphor for a field of central discourses that emerged in the nineteenth century which operated to regulate behaviour. His approach to Victorian discourses relating to sex proposed that the taboo around sexuality was only possible because sexual practice was constantly being monitored through speech and texts (Foucault 1979). By treating sex as a taboo subject, the Victorians involuntarily expressed the centrality of questions of sexual management and regulation in everyday life.

Under Mao, Chinese society revolved around the panopticon of the Party and, above all, the eye of the leader. Mao died in 1976. Since his death, the trend in Chinese society has been towards general, albeit conditional, liberalization, with the retention of the Party structure as the dominant force in Chinese society. It is easy to exaggerate the strength of liberalization. The Tiananmen Square massacre in 1989 displayed to the disbelieving eyes of the world that reactionary elements persisted in government after Mao's death. However, since Tiananmen, even hardline Party leaders and officials have realized that globalization fatally restricts their power to act as they please.

The web is one important aspect of globalization. Its growth in China makes it harder for the Party elite to impose central control. The difficulties of policing the web in communist China are twofold. In the first place, Western servers cannot be effectively banished from Chinese cyber space. As such, Chinese citizens receive exposure to a variety of views about China that openly contradict the version portrayed by the Chinese leadership. The second policing problem is that domestic sites have a high capacity to resist detection. They have the ability to change identity overnight and disrupt central servers virally. These combined problems with the central management of information mean that a second Cultural Revolution in China is improbable.

Of course, precisely because there are inherent difficulties in policing the web, there is also a dark side to the expansion of the internet. Its growth created new opportunities for the development of spam-email and internet viruses. The instructions for making the bombs used by the London bombers in 2005 are still freely available on the web, and terrorists of all persuasions can refer to them. So are militant anti-Christian and anti-Western sites that encourage incitement. Internet growth also provided new channels for exploiting and developing pornography, paedophile rings, cultural stereotyping and fanning the flames of racial and religious hatred. Unequivocally, as with nearly all technologies, there is a downside to the internet. Yet the sheer cultural presence of this technology in just ten years is so remarkable that it is impossible for the billion or so of us who are regular users to imagine a world without it.

Doing Cultural Studies 3: The mobile phone

Over the same decade or so, the development of mobile phones provided a parallel revolution in mass communication and popular culture. Texting and photo-exchange created many new cultural genres. Text dating emerged as a new popular phenomenon. The use of mobile phones as cameras became a significant means of exchanging family photographs. Phone cameras were a valuable resource for the police in the hunt for the identities of the twin cells of terrorist bombers who attacked London on 7/7 and 21/7 in 2005. Mobile phones freed mass information and entertainment from fixed and dedicated sites of broadcasting and reception, making them more or less ubiquitous. In the last decade, mobile phones have moved from being an option in youth culture to a standard requirement. As a teenager, you can't be taken seriously by your peers unless you are connected to a pay-as-you-go or monthly rental system. New cultural genres emerged around mobile phone brands and service like Ericsson, Nokia, Motorola, Vodafone and Orange. The refinement of web browsers turned the mobile into a type of newspaper, offering instant breaking stories in any location. Among the individuals and groups that use mobile phones, the choice of pay-as-you-go deals over line rental arrangements became important indicators of lifestyle and cultural status. The new mobile multi-media services became sought after status symbols and thus a novel element in cultural politics. For these individuals and groups, the mobile is not merely a communication device, it is an accessory of cultural identification and recognition.

As with the internet, there is another side to mobile phone use. Mobile phones are associated with new types of intrusion into public space. On public trains and buses they have been unilaterally employed as an extension of both office and domestic space, so much so that transport companies have been prevailed upon to introduce 'quiet zones' for passengers who want to preserve their privacy. Their use on aeroplanes interferes with signalling and is a flying hazard. Companies send customers unsolicited text messages advertising new products so that the phone is turned into a receptacle for junk mail. In addition, texts and phone calls can be monitored and copied by the police and other external bodies, for surveillance purposes. Yet the advantages of mobile phones clearly outweigh the disadvantages. They offer a versatile new way of sending and receiving information. Although they are widely condemned for spreading 'contentless culture' (empty conversations about nothing), they also carry immense potential for extending and refining active citizenship.

Multiple modernities

Because modern culture is super-dynamic, the curriculum in Cultural Studies must, to some extent, be in a state of flux. A proviso needs to be added here. Although it is perfectly correct to describe modern culture as categorically super-dynamic, concrete cultural analysis reveals different rates of velocity among groups. This is because people are situated in various and diverse relations of scarcity with respect to economic, political, technological, cultural and communication resources and stimuli. It follows that some groups will be more practised and therefore more accustomed to living with dynamism than others. For example, a clerical worker employed by EMI records will probably have less direct experience of cultural dynamism than Chris Martin, the lead singer and main songwriter in Coldplay. The former is more likely to be reliant on public transport, inhabit restricted dwelling space, seldom engage in long distance travel and have unlimited access to the full range of telecommunications in network society. Nonetheless, the clerical worker is no less part of a cultural context in which dynamism and change are more accentuated general features of ordinary life than in traditional society.

Because of this it is perhaps preferable to use the term 'multiple modernities' to refer to the diverse patterns of lived experience in relation to the velocity of life in modern culture. It is not just that we are all different. Our differences are patterned by the relationship we have to economic, cultural, political and social scarcity. The adjective 'multiple' is designed to recognize the plural character of cultural, technological, economic and social experience. It is a defence against over-egging the uniformity of culture in our accounts of contemporary culture.

Multiple modernities can be studied in nearly every large city in the West. This is because one aspect of postwar globalization is the rise of multicultural society. The ethnic, sexual and religious mix of modern culture makes it hazardous to attribute homogeneity or unity to national cultures. Cultural and postcolonial theorists argue that it is now essential to examine cultures in terms of 'difference' and 'the other'. Within Western national traditions considerable variation with respect to ethnic belonging, sexual identity and religious belief are tolerated. Cultural analysis needs to be sensitive to these variations and consistently defend 'multiple modernities' as the primary condition of contemporary culture.

In turn, this raises new questions about the nature of cultural belonging and solidarity. While it is doubtless true that there never was only one way of being British, American or Australian, there has never been as much acknowledged internal diversity and variation as now. Students of modern culture, then, not only face cultural forms that are subject to rapid change, they confront historically unprecedented levels of cultural differentiation and variety.

3

Culture is Structured
Like a Language

Because modern culture is in a state of flux, Cultural Studies needs to be unusually open to the possibility of constant revision. Despite this, there are some concepts that are fundamental. One of them is communication. Communication is pivotal to Cultural Studies because language is the principal means of exchanging and developing meaning. Although the discipline did not follow Saussure's structural linguistics (1915) in a slavish way, it was profoundly influenced by his famous idea concerning language and meaning. That is, meaning is the expression of the inter-relation between a term in its textual or acoustic form (*signifier*) and the concept to which the term refers (*signified*). For Saussure, the relationship between the signifier and the signified is *arbitrary*. In other words there is no inherent reason why the word 'cat' refers to the quadrupedal, carnivorous mammal with smooth fur and retractable claws. It is just that way because the meaning of the term happens to be so positioned in relation to other combinations of signifier and sign in the Anglophone system of language.

Cultural Studies took over this idea by contending that culture is structured like a language. Conceptually speaking, this is a provocative and instructive way of thinking about history, power, representation and identity. For example, there is no inherent reason why Patrick Tillman chose to be an American patriot or why SPC Charles Garner, PTE Lynndi England and other military prison personnel maltreated inmates at the Abu Ghraib military camp. One might point to their family histories, their schooling, the subcultures to which they are attached, the seductive authority that military culture has for some people and other social, cultural, political and economic factors. But the personal identities that emerged from these factors were not *fatefully* decreed, rather they were the outcome of the material and symbolic positioning of individuals in the interrelationship between cultural, political, social and economic forces. The 'real' course of their biographies was constantly shaped by the interplay and penetration of cultural codes, themes and representations.

Similarly, there is no inherent reason why someone is a fan of Real Madrid or the New York Yankees; why one person is a devotee of opera and another of the blues; why one person is a fan of the novels of Saul Bellow and another, those of J.K. Rowling; or why some people regard Princess Diana as the ultimate victim, while others condemn her as an arch manipulator.

Our identities are of course shaped by genetic inheritance. But they are also culturally coded and themed through communication and representation. Of course, individuals possess conscience and power, but culture positions them in relation to economic, social, political and cultural resources that nudge preferences in favoured directions. Indeed, among the best reasons for doing Cultural Studies is to divest yourself of the notion of absolute personal uniqueness and to alert you to the role of cultural codes, themes and representations of individualism in constructing your own point of view and behaviour.

There are many ways of being in the world. Cultural Studies challenges you to re-envisage your life and relations in your community, in connection with the cultural, social, economic and political factors that give your sense of identity its particular form and content. Discovering the repressed and coded parts of yourself and the communities to which you are attached is part and parcel of the discipline. So is locating the part of representation, theming and coding in sustaining popular ideas of paramount reality.

The imaginary

Generally, this has been developed against the grain of cultural arrangements that insist upon highly selective, rigidly disciplined hierarchies of culture, which is why Cultural Studies is usually thought of as a critical activity, an activity that rocks the boat. Think of racist cultures that portray one race as the zenith of human development, or religious cultures that purport to be in touch with one sacred truth and therefore demand unwavering obedience. By examining these cultures from the perspective of representation, coding and theming, Cultural Studies often clashes with established interests.

While it has been expressed in diverse ways, the imaginative goal of Cultural Studies is to seek to transcend these hierarchies. The philosopher Charles Taylor (2004) maintains that the semi-hidden world, the world of subcultural difference and cultural possibility, is the inevitable corollary of cultural hierarchy. It offers no escape from the animal world of pain, betrayal, jealousy, suffering and death. Nonetheless, through the stories, poems, art and criticism that it nurtures it provides a necessary narrative counterpoint of alternative solidarity to mainstream cultures.

In the time of the fatwa issued by the Ayatollah upon the life of the Anglo-Indian novelist Salman Rushdie, BBC Radio interviewed Rushdie. The fatwa had been decreed because the novelist was held to have blasphemed against the Prophet in his novel *The Satanic Verses* (1988). Published during the long Thatcherite neo-liberal adventure in Britain, the book is indeed critical of many aspects of Islam. Yet it is also a ferocious attack upon British double-standards and racism, especially as they are embodied in the language of the state, with respect to class and race. Distaste for this culture is a long-abiding feature of Rushdie's writing, although in most of his other work it is explored in the colonial milieux. In the programme Rushdie was asked why he chose to stay in Britain given his profound misgivings about the history and practice of the British state, the persistence of racism and class control. He replied that it was because he felt connected to 'another Britain', the Britain that links Blake, Shelley, Orwell, C.L.R. James, Ken Loach, Mike Leigh, the Beatles, Erin Pizzey, the Clash, Morrissey and Pete Doherty. We might extend this to an American context in which 'another America' is represented by figures like Allen Ginsberg, Bob Dylan, Kurt Cobain, Johnny Depp, Robert Crumb, Spike Lee, Jim Jarmusch, Lydia Lunch, Karen Finlay, Patty Smith, John Sayles, Hunter S. Thompson and bell hooks; or to an Australian setting wherein 'another Australia' can be found in figures like Jack Lindsay, Bernard Smith, Ned Kelly, Banjo Patterson, Ian Chappell, Betty Churcher, Lois O'Donoghue and Dawn Casey.

These are illustrations of what Taylor (2004) means by *the social imaginary*, it is the 'other cultures', the cultures of *difference* and *possibility*, that are the inevitable complements of cultures of domination. Through these largely unstructured, informalized cultures we imagine our social existence, how we fit together with others, how things work between ourselves and others and, crucially, how things *ought* to be (Taylor 2004: 23–4). They are latent with the capacity for cultural intervention and, as such, are a primary resource for transformation in modern culture.

Cultural Studies, then, is about appreciating how power shapes meaning, and through this, liberating yourself from the grip of some of its tentacles; learning to understand the strength and popularity of myth, but being committed to demystifying the world; connecting with the remarkable pace of change in modern society, but not allowing yourself to be overwhelmed by it; and understanding how representation and theming operate to *position* you to hold fast to particular outlooks and values. It contributes to an enlarged perspective of citizenship, but it also helps you to better understand yourself and those around you. At its best, Cultural Studies is an emancipatory practice designed to widen your perspective about the various ways in which we are interconnected with and divided from each other, nationally, globally and historically, and the role of coding and representation in establishing a shared sense of paramount reality and also of cultural inclusion, exclusion and difference. Beyond this it also alerts us to the situated character of poverty, marginality and social exclusion. Far from being inevitable, these conditions reflect the interweaving of cultural, social, economic and political forces and the positioning of individuals in relation to them.

The 3 D's

Cultural Studies is not party political. Historically, it has deep roots in the Marxist tradition. However, it is implausible today to maintain that it is still beholden to that tradition. From a largely British base, the globalization of Cultural Studies, after the 1970s, has multiplied the fronts in which emancipatory practice is understood and pursued. The discipline has its share of traditional left-wing activists, but postcolonialists, feminists and post-feminists, queer theorists, postmodernists, cyber space theorists, men's studies writers, anti-capitalists, planetary humanists, deconstructionists and anti-essentialists are also among its number.

Although there are many differences between them, most would agree with Cornell West's identification of emancipatory practice in Cultural Studies with 'a new politics of difference' (1992). West goes on to argue that this politics is defined by '3 D's':

1 *Deconstruction* – a critical attitude to the primary dichotomies in language and culture which operate to entrench divisions and fetter identity. West has in mind oppositions like black/white, male/female,

American/Arab, which culturally and linguistically privilege the first term over the other. Deconstruction focuses on the interrogation of cultural meaning in order to expose the political underpinnings of common unexamined cultural divisions.

2 *Demythologization* – revealing how cultural reality and a sense of the shared past is coded and represented by myth. Since myth is always the articulation of power, demythologization logically points to the exposure of the social, economic and cultural interests behind myth.

3 *Demystification* – linking the exposure of myth, manipulation and power to active cultural politics and cultural policy. Students of Cultural Studies should play an active role in disseminating knowledge to communities in order to encourage activism and the development of new cultural forms which recognize the need for distributive justice, social inclusion and empowerment.

This 'politics of difference' continuously raises questions of coding, representation, theming and ultimately *power*. The *iconoclastic* association is crucial. Cultural Studies exists to break moulds. It is committed to releasing human potential that has been constrained by the blind forces of culture, society, economics and politics. This means taking a position on questions of economic, social and political justice. But it also means maintaining an open and engaged attitude to technological, scientific and cultural change. Culture counts because it is the primary means through which we communicate and influence reality. Indeed, we cannot comprehend reality, let alone take steps to act upon it, without using cultural codes, traditions and representations. Culture is therefore located at the fulcrum of the human condition. This is why the study of it is not only of practical significance, but also a contribution to the process of human enlargement.

4

Zeroing in on Culture

More than ever before, we are aware that the cultural positions that we convey are conditioned by *processed representations* produced by advertising, photography, television, film, radio, newspapers, magazines and music. This has partly contributed to a *dematerialized, depersonalized* relationship with social and cultural reality. For example, we no longer rely on news and views about the world simply by word of mouth via our parents, local community and friendship networks. Even the radio and television have been surpassed by the internet and mobile phone web browsers. Of course, kith and kin networks and radio and television remain important channels in producing our sense of everyday cultural reality. But we also inhabit a media-sphere of images, sound-bites and sequences of mass communications which support our understanding of social, cultural, political and economic reality. The media pattern representation and identity in complex ways. Cultural Studies explores the ways in which meanings are communicated and identities are represented and themed.

Of course, it is also much more than this. In societies that revolve around mass communications, in which a good deal of cultural life occurs via the news, cues and prompts of behaviour perpetuated by the media, the capitalist state (ultimately dedicated to defending and bolstering market society) and multinational corporations, the emphasis upon the application of images and styling in the construction of identity and behaviour is pronounced. However, if our identities and behaviour are *just* matters of cultural styling where would personal will figure? Cultural Studies examines culture as inherently *political*. It does so, among other reasons, to rebut the notion that humans are docile, plastic creatures whose opinions, values, beliefs and appearance are shaped by the various forces that comprise *the culture industry*. The latter may be defined as the aggregate of state departments, advertising agencies, television companies, music corporations, film multinationals and press corporations. Their power in framing meaning has been used to argue that the culture industry dominates popular culture.[1] Against this, Cultural Studies insists upon investigating culture as a perpetual mix of both force and resistance.

The origins of Cultural Studies

The academic study of popular culture commenced in the 1950s, was institutionalized between the mid-1960s and late 1980s, and became a cause célèbre thereafter, especially when it was attached to new degree programmes in Media, Communication and Cultural Studies. Popular culture *was* studied before the 1950s, but in a fashion that unintentionally impeded its development. Three traditions were particularly significant.

(1) *Elitism* is associated with writers like Matthew Arnold (1869) and Edward Tylor (1874) in the nineteenth century and, in the twentieth century, T.S. Eliot (1948) and the peculiar variant developed by F.R. Leavis (1948, 1962), with its hair-raising vision that humanistic values stood on the brink of being obliterated by technology. While there are many important differences between them, these writers tended to dismiss popular culture as philistine, vulgar and regressive. They were intolerant of difference, and sceptical of the validity of cultures of resistance based upon issues of class, race or gender. In general, they subscribed to an evolutionary model of culture by which, to paraphrase Matthew Arnold, what is thought and said in 'Society', meaning 'High Society', is assumed to be the *best* that can be thought and said. Even when low born refugees, like D.H. Lawrence, the son of a Nottinghamshire collier, were recognized as entering the ranks of the exalted, their contribution was summarily amalgamated into 'the great tradition', in Leavis's phrase, rather than articulating oppositional interests and cultures. Only the oracles of 'sophisticated culture', usually located in the Humanities faculties of ancient universities, were thought to be in a position to correctly assess cultural worth. This was a hierarchical, patrician model that identified high culture with the ancient manual technologies of writing, painting

and drama. Machine technologies like photography, and later television, film and sound recording, were mistrusted, precisely because, with training and practice, anyone could theoretically become adept in them. They belonged to the culture of everyman. As such, they were associated with access rather than contest, and inclusion rather than excellence.

The political agenda posed by this position was obscure. In Arnold, Tylor and Eliot, it veered towards an aspirational model in which the brightest among the ranks of the lower orders would be encouraged to emulate the beliefs and practices of elite achievement. The rational recreation movement after the 1870s sought to apply this in sport, leisure, the arts and science. Leavis's position was more embattled. Bizarre as it seems now, he was convinced that 'sophisticated culture' was on the brink of a gathering tsunami of cultural decline and he proposed that the university English department should be transformed into a bastion of 'sophisticated culture'. Here, intellectuals, disassociated from established social interests, would construct the ramparts and erect the barricades to defend the values of humanism, while leaving 'the culture of the people' either to go hang or to be 'improved' by cultural leaders. As the twentieth century progressed, and mass access to education increased, together with improvements in mass communication which broadened information space relating to difference, non-conformity and power, all versions of the elitist approach gradually became unable to defend themselves from the charge that they were actually nothing more than a type of cultural domination.

(2) *Urban Social Anthropology*, in Britain, was associated above all with the Mass-Observation studies into everyday life conducted between 1937 and 1955. Founded by Tom Harrisson, Charles Madge and Humphrey Jennings, Mass-Observation organized teams of paid investigators to record people's behaviour and conversation in a range of public settings. The methods used included participant observation, questionnaires, interviews, open-ended descriptions and the analysis of printed ephemera. In addition, some 500 men and women kept diaries of their behaviour and sent them to Mass-Observation on a monthly basis. The subjects addressed included, 'Astrology and Spiritualism', 'Commercial Advertising', 'Commodities', 'Games and Jigsaws', 'Holidays', 'Leisure', 'Live Entertainment', 'Personal Appearance and Clothes', 'Shopping' and 'Sport'. Mass-Observation was partly influenced by the surrealist principle of discovering strangeness and beauty in the ordinary. However, it was unable to liberate itself from the native British tradition of dogged, but theoretically uninspired, empiricism or fact-finding. The Archive,

now housed in the Special Collections library at Sussex University, comprises an Aladdin's cave of unique, fascinating data on everyday life in Britain between 1937 and 1955, but the theoretical and political dimensions are notably understated.

The Chicago School in America provided a significant counterpoint to the British tradition. The work of Thomas and Zaniecki (1929), Park, Burgess and Mackenzie (1925), Cressey (1932), Zorbaugh (1929) and Whyte (1943) argued that urban-industrial culture must be taken seriously. The study of community life in Muncie, Indiana, conducted by Robert and Helen Lynd (1928), used social survey methods to examine everyday life. They divided social life into six segments: Getting a Living; Making a Home; Training the Young; Using Leisure; Engaging in Religious Practices; and Engaging in Community Activities. They argued that class is central to culture. They held a progressive view of social development in as much as they believed that modernization would erode class differences. This led them to minimize the importance of conflict and difference and exaggerate the reformist effect of technology and the welfare state.

All of this American work contributed greatly to our knowledge of Western popular culture. However, a general weakness of it was that it was unable to rise above a descriptive level. As with the British tradition, the theoretical and political dimensions of analysing popular culture were largely left fallow.

(3) *Mass Society/Mass Culture* was most influential between the late 1940s and late 1960s, and its defining feature was the proposition that everyday life is subject to thorough-going manipulation. The result of this is the standardization and regimentation of popular culture. Theoretically, there was an important division in what constituted what might be called the primary *agent* of manipulation. The American approach, associated with the writings of David Riesman (1950) and Vance Packard (1957, 1959) pointed to the *corporation* as the key. Through advertising and control of the mass media, American popular culture was being engineered to fulfil corporate goals. The German (Frankfurt School) approach, associated with Adorno and Horkheimer (1944) and Marcuse (1964), attributed decisive influence to class and rationalization. Class control of 'the culture industry' (mass media and organized popular entertainment) and the application of rational, bureaucratic principles to everyday life was held to produce mass conformity.

This tradition highlighted the significance of the new forms of representation produced by the mass media in the organization of mass culture. Advertising, radio, television, film and popular print culture were no longer regarded as separate from popular culture. On the contrary, they were now regarded as *informing* popular culture, providing everyday life with packaged identities and blueprints of lifestyles.

On the whole, and especially in the Frankfurt approach, politics and theory were more pronounced in this tradition. However, it tended to give accentuated importance to domination and manipulation over resistance and opposition. In addition, there was an oddly detached style to the analysis of popular culture. So much so that one observer complained of the Frankfurt researchers that they reminded him of guests in the 'Grand Hotel Abyss', loftily observing the capitulation of mass culture to class manipulation from a position of insulated comfort (Lukacs 1962). Certainly, both the American and Frankfurt traditions did not involve committed political activism. For the later generation who forged the discipline of Cultural Studies as we now know it, this was a source of regret, and perhaps a spur to making politics pivotal in the business of cultural analysis.

Postwar Cultural Studies

Today, Cultural Studies is truly global. In the division of labour, the USA is now the dominant force. The work of Dave Andrews, Stanley Aronowitz, Paula Chakravartty, C.L. Cole, Michael Curtin, Susan G. Davis, Susan Douglas, John Dowling, Philomena Essed, Rosaq-Linda Fregoso, Faye Ginsburg, Herman Gray, Michael Hanchard, Fredric Jameson, Doug Kellner, Laura Kipnis, Marian Beevi Lam, Cameron McCarthy, Anne McLintock, Lisa McLaughlin, Jorge Mariscal, Randy Martin, George Marux, Rob Nixon, Vorris Nunley, Constance Penley, Dana Polan, Ellen Seiter and Ella Shohat – to name but a few – is driving Cultural Studies into exciting new avenues of research and reflection. This work has been hugely influential, especially in the emerging and developing Latin American countries where the work of American writers like James Carey and Nestor Garcia Canclini is widely embraced. Australia, Hong Kong, India, South Korea and Canada are developing distinctive and durable traditions that expose the limitations of Eurocentric/American dominated approaches. Researchers in these countries have seized the baton of Cultural Studies and run with it in unfamiliar and exciting ways.

However, the baton was created elsewhere. Since this book is not a survey of international research traditions in Cultural Studies but an attempt to explain its origins and key themes I will not try to focus on the global division of labour in the subject. Instead I will confine myself to the task of trying to clarify the trajectory of development of the subject. For this trajectory was the crucial force in stimulating research programmes throughout the world.

The postwar birth of Cultural Studies in universities was a very British affair. One of the unintended consequences of the Second World War was to erode class barriers and promote egalitarianism. This was symbolized in the election of the Labour government in 1945. Committed to the nationalization of central heights of the economy and the creation of the welfare state, the Labour government introduced an unprecedented programme of state investment in public life.

Initially, the discipline of Cultural Studies crystallized around the expansion of secondary and tertiary education which extended ordinary people's participation in formal education; the construction of the welfare state which posed new questions of civil entitlements and rights; the achievement of full employment and the affluent society which increased real wages and expanded consumer culture, leisure and tourism; the rise of television as the most popular form of leisure and the emergence of pop music as a compact, intense and often exhilarating expression of youth culture; the development of the paperback book market, symbolized by the swift ascent of Penguin Books as the entertainer and educator of the poor man and woman, increased access to literature, philosophy and social analysis; the sponsorship on radio and television of new forms of popular comedy which ridiculed the class ladder and the paraphernalia of privilege (*The Goon Show*, *Beyond the Fringe*, *Hancock's Half Hour*, *Round The Horne*, *That Was The Week That Was* and in the 1970s *Monty Python*); the extraordinary burst of creativity in theatre, television and film from the likes of Harold Pinter, Edward Bond, Alan Sillitoe, David Mercer, Dennis Potter, Ken Loach and Trevor Griffiths, which unapologetically addressed issues of working-class life and economic and cultural inequality; and the growth of multi-ethnicity provoked by the national shortage of cheap domestic labour and the influx of immigrant labour from the Commonwealth. Nor was this all.

The postwar settlement gave the USA not merely a military presence in Western Europe but a cultural one as well, through American military bases. During this time, the potentially harmful, levelling effects of the Americanization of British and European culture was a constant refrain in the media. In a foretaste of the debate on globalization, commentators ventilated on the fragility of nation-state boundaries, the helplessness of traditional British (and European) customs to showy American alternatives, and the infiltration of monetary values into leisure and sport. This many-sided cultural, economic and political transformation in British/ European life widened popular awareness of cultural difference and raised new questions of cultural integrity. Cultural Studies, then, did not instigate cultural transformation. Rather, it is best understood as part of a seismic shift in the structure of British and European society.

In the 1960s and 1970s Cultural Studies began to be established in the university system, notably at the Centre for Contemporary Cultural Studies at the University of Birmingham. The field seemed more relevant than other branches of the Humanities and Social Sciences because it unapologetically engaged with popular culture. 'Field' is perhaps the most appropriate term to use, since Cultural Studies was always inter- ested in breaking down disciplinary boundaries and encouraging the cross-pollination of concepts, theories and traditions. Instead of regard- ing popular culture as uninteresting and subordinate in the manner of the elitist tradition, a documentary resource *à la* the Mass-Observation Group or a victim of class domination bearing the scar tissue of manipu- lation, as tended to be the case with the Frankfurt School approach, Cultural Studies explored popular culture as bursting with creativity, invention and vitality. At the same time, it recognized a domestic postwar heritage in the subject consisting of the writings of Richard Hoggart, E.P. Thompson and Raymond Williams.

Richard Hoggart's (1958) famous study of the working-class district of Hunslet in the city of Leeds is widely acknowledged to be a catalyst in the formation of Cultural Studies as an academic discipline. It boldly sought to rid working-class culture of the patronizing views of the elite. It examined the spatial contours of cultural content and form that practi- cally engaged with inequality without capitulating to the authority of ruling strata. E.P. Thompson (1963) did the same thing for working-class history, but with an incomparably richer range of cultural data and a deeper Marxist perspective. Raymond Williams (1963, 1965) argued that the culture of the oppressed possessed aesthetic, moral and political value and denigrated the condescension of elite culture. He developed a position of *cultural materialism* which analysed cultural themes and representations in relation to the actual means and conditions of their production. He also developed the concepts of the 'selective tradition' in culture, by which is meant the cultural positions and artefacts that are 'automatically' thought to be worth preserving or venerating, and 'struc- ture of feeling' which refers to the cultural sensibility of a generation or era through which personal experience is conducted and cultural experi- ence accumulates. These notions are now so widely accepted in Cultural

Studies and, for that matter, culture at large, that Williams's achievement is all too easily glossed over (Jones 2004).

These three writers were particularly significant in making the British take popular culture seriously. It cannot be emphasized enough that their task was helped immensely by the structural changes taking place in British society. The shift of resources to the welfare state, the consequent revitalization of debates about the nature of citizenship rights, the rise in real incomes which followed full employment and postwar reconstruction and the explosion of the new technologies of television, the transistor radio, tape recorders and portable record players, transformed the terms of trade for analysing popular culture. Working-class people and ethnic minorities were more visible and more mobile because they were generally richer and possessed greater access to the new electronic media than their ancestors had acquired in relation to print culture. As a result, the subject of popular culture could no longer be safely confined by the media to workers' housing districts and the cheap tabloid newspapers and magazines. It now occupied the vanguard of culture, politics and society.

This was part of what Williams (1965) calls 'the long revolution' in technological, democratic and cultural relations. He understood this to reach back for over four centuries to encompass the challenge to structures of authority based around the monarch, the growth of the free press, the rise of mass literacy, the creation of a reading public and the emergence of radio and television. For Williams, the 'whole way of life' of a people is bound up with systems of communication, learning and representation. Unlike traditional societies, these systems are subject to perpetual change and transformation because technology, culture and democracy change, often in ways that are unforeseen. The concept of the long revolution captures very well the emergence of various active, material forces that create a sense of culture that is external to individuals and groups, but which arise from the countless willed actions of individuals and groups.

Hoggart, Thompson and Williams were very British figures. Their data was mostly drawn from British culture and British history. But the mechanisms of cultural positioning and the formations of class, power and ideology that they wrote about were transferable to other countries and regions. When Thompson (1963) wrote his great book about the *English* working class with its powerful descriptions of elite condescension and working-class resistance and challenge, the mechanisms that he analysed found their counterpart in the USA, the British commonwealth and many other market based urban-industrial cultures. It was the practice of Cultural Studies to address what the established disciplines had ignored or treated with indifference that made the knowledge base and the whole style of analysis attractive to students in different parts of the world. An additional factor in globalizing the field was the migration and repatriation of key figures from the Birmingham circle to the USA and the commonwealth. Hazel Carby, Dick Hebdige and Paul Gilroy (although he returned to the UK in 2005) moved to the USA. Larry Grossberg returned to the USA and has some claim to being Hall's foremost American disciple. Graeme Turner returned to Australia and wrote one of the most insightful early critical assessments of British Cultural Studies (Turner 1990). There is a sense in which these writers conducted their careers through a dialogue with Hoggart, Thompson, Williams and Hall but crucially inflected it through an engagement with local conditions in North America and Australasia.

Culture is ordinary

Raymond Williams (1958) originally formulated the proposition that 'culture is ordinary'. This deceptively simple remark contained a twofold presupposition of some complexity. Firstly, Williams was concerned to divest elitist propaganda of the principle that the *ordinary* has no cultural value. Working-class cultural content and form was examined as operating within a context of unequal resource distribution, and even *gaining* cultural space and moral/political authority through struggle.

Secondly, Williams sought to combat the view that culture is compartmentalized from the rest of life, as if one engages in it only after the day's work or on the weekend. Instead, he argued that all of life is immersed in culture and politics. One can no more escape being involved with culture than one can avoid eating and drinking. Indeed eating and drinking are themselves cultural forms which vary comparatively and historically. There was, then, recognition of enormous variety in cultural form and content. Culture may be studied in relation to traditions and practices referring to lifestyle, work, school, music, art, environment, dwelling space, fashion, science, movies and much else besides. The variety of form and content is one of the reasons why the subject was so swiftly recognized to be relevant and vital: the changing urban-industrial world and how these changes are communicated and represented is your subject. It is also why Cultural Studies is challenging, for potentially there is no barrier to what can be investigated.

An important corollary of Williams's argument that culture is ordinary is his proposition that culture is *selective*. This was partly designed to run the gauntlet over the portrayal of elite culture as the zenith of human achievement by sensitizing readers to the various concrete and symbolic limitations in the content and form of elite culture. But it also highlighted the importance of the physical and symbolic *location* of culture. For Williams, far from being exclusively a matter of art and belles-lettres, culture is integral to the 'way of life' of a particular people in a specific spatial location with concrete, unequal access to economic, cultural and political resources. This perspective of *cultural materialism* takes it for granted that there is considerable variation in cultural form and content within national populations, but it makes no presuppositions about the *value* of cultural difference.

5

The Four 'Moments' in Cultural Studies

In order to understand Cultural Studies, we must clarify how it has developed and changed over the last forty years. It is appropriate to take forty years as the relevant time-span because the first academic department of Cultural Studies, the Centre for Contemporary Cultural Studies, was founded in the University of Birmingham in 1964. We already know that Cultural Studies is marked by significant variety in methods, theories and politics. The question is: How can we make this variety manageable for the purpose of comprehension? One way of doing so is by framing the postwar development of the subject in terms of four 'moments'. The term 'moment' is widely used in the discipline and is preferable to the more mechanical terms of 'juncture' or 'stages'. 'Moment' conveys the impression of process, and overlapping streams and cross-currents in which debate and research is buoyed forward in a decisive front.

Broadly speaking, I propose, there have been four such 'moments' in the history of Cultural Studies: *National-Popular*, *Textual-Representational*, *Global/Post-Essentialism* and *Governmentality/Policy*. Each has brought differing criteria, objectives and preoccupations to the fore in the study of culture. The National-Popular uses Marxism, Classical sociological methodologies and a blend of continental philosophy to explore questions of youth and popular subcultures. The Textual-Representational employs literary analysis to examine popular culture, everyday life, the media and film. The Global/Post-Essentialism moment focuses on questions of identity, especially identities that have been marginalized by capitalism such as ethnic minorities, postcolonial cultures, gays and lesbians. A fourth moment, the moment of

Governmentality/Policy, which is still emerging, concentrates on the institutions and policies that produce and govern cultural practice. In describing these moments, I want to re-emphasize their overlapping and emerging character rather than unintentionally give any suggestion of linear progression and closure. Thus, in each moment, aspects of the other three can be readily identified, but they are underscored in comparison with the defining feature that characterizes the time.

National-Popular (1956–84)

The term 'national-popular' derives from the writings of the Marxist cultural theorist Antonio Gramsci (1971). He emphasized the importance of culture and politics partly against the vulgar Marxist notion of *economic determinism*. This notion held that economic structure is foundational and determines relations in the *superstructure* of society, namely politics, culture, education and religion. Gramsci's approach raised new questions about the formation of groups within the field of politics. This shifted discussion away from the role of class struggle and economics in social change. The change in direction focused on the character of the new groups in the field of politics and culture, their relationships with one another and their influence in shaping national-popular relations. Culture and politics were redefined as a *complex unity* of relations in which the balance of power involved multiple points of force and resistance.

Various consequences followed from this in relation to understanding how culture is located and operates. Classical Marxism presents culture as situated in a framework that is defined by ideology and the relations of production. Marx argued that the ideas of the ruling class are the ruling ideas in society. Ideology operates to integrate the dominant class. It applies repression and force to marginalize or erase the interests of subordinate classes. Ideology works best when relations of domination and subordination are *culturally reproduced*. That is, when a historically specific system of power is presented as inevitable or without an alternative. It follows that an important aim in the classical Marxism of class struggle is to unmask the ideology of the ruling class.

In societies where civil rights have been extended, and notions of parliamentary democratic rights apply, the concept of ideology is too crude. The concept of hegemony recognizes this. Like ideology, hegemony dictates a framework in which class struggle is waged. However, it operates through *positioning* and *persuasion*. It locates groups in relation to scarce resources and provides a plausible justification for the arrangement, that is a justification that is accepted or tolerated by groups who gain advantage from it, but who are nonetheless positioned as dependent. Sometimes positioning is given by awarding groups recognition and rights that they did not possess before. Sometimes it involves making concessions to forces that successfully challenge the status quo. Repression and force are only used as a last resort and typically with the *consent* of the majority.

Gramsci argued that hegemony is the expression of a *power bloc* rather than a unified ruling class. By this term he meant a set of associations and alliances of ruling interests that is ascendant in culture and society and seeks to engineer national-popular dominance. The concept therefore recognizes divisions of interest within the power bloc and that ascendancy requires constant negotiation and bargaining both within the leading power bloc and within subordinate groups and classes. Gramsci distinguished between 'the war of position' in which groups and classes struggle to gain recognition in civil society and the 'war of manoeuvre' in which the focus turns upon transforming recognition into power. In this approach to culture the state is pivotal. Controlling the state means having access to the central levers of power over the national-popular.

During this moment in Cultural Studies the subject sought to illuminate this balance of integration, and the multiple points of force and resistance linked to it, through historical and concrete analysis. It took over Gramsci's concept of the *organic intellectual* which referred to an intellectual labourer situated at the cutting edge of ideas, who is committed to disseminating them among the people so as to promote social change. In so doing the aim was to collaborate in partnership with men and women in ordinary culture to transform the fundamental cultural, social and political categories in popular thought and action in a socialist direction. Much of the inspiration behind this task derived from what was perceived as the exhaustion of orthodox party politics. The bankruptcy of imperialism was dramatically exposed by the Suez crisis of 1956; but the Soviet invasion of Hungary in the same year persuaded many on the Left that the Stalinist version of communism was no better.

Throughout this period the arbitrary character of meaning, the textual form of cultural behaviour and the slippage between signs and signifiers were, of course, prominent themes. But the work that was given real kudos, the work that got people talking and arguing, explicitly connected these themes to questions of the distribution and legitimation of political power, the marginalization of popular culture and increasing the power of the people. Following Gramsci, the focus of these questions was the 'national-popular', that is, national-popular cultures and the state systems associated with them, which are the arena of political and cultural struggle. Correspondingly, the global dimensions of culture and power were under-theorized. To begin with, this work outwardly concentrated upon the subject of the communication processes in the mass media. Yet it soon moved on to the question of class and eventually issues of sexual and racial domination.

In Britain, the practical and symbolic pivot of organized Cultural Studies during this period was the Birmingham Centre for Contemporary Cultural Studies (CCCS) opened in 1964. The Centre occupies a legendary place in the history of Cultural Studies. Richard Hoggart was the founding director of the Centre in the University of Birmingham. His original vision for it was of a tripartite division of teaching and research activities between literary, historical-philosophical and sociological questions. Much of the excitement of working and studying there between 1964 and 1979, which is generally agreed to be the Centre's heyday, was due to the collaborative spirit of teaching and research cultivated between teachers and students (who for most of the Centre's history were exclusively postgraduates). Staff in the Centre saw themselves as working in a laboratory. They encouraged students to be instrumental in inventing and developing the curriculum. The interest in the unconventional, the marginalized, the ordinary and the repressed led to questioning the validity of academic borders and making a virtue of trans-disciplinarity. In particular, students of Cultural Studies borrowed from English, Sociology, Social Theory, Anthropology and Philosophy to develop their approach. The sense of being unshackled by academic precedent, being inventive about cultural study and regarding many of the traditional disciplines as politically naive was fundamental. This echoes back to a point already made, namely that from the outset, organized Cultural Studies was about *breaking the mould*. The self-image of researchers and students was to ask questions that were not being asked in other disciplines and to take seriously what was elsewhere dismissed as trifling or of no importance in cultural relations.

Initially, the focus of research was upon the ordinary, lived culture of the working class. This mirrored Hoggart's pioneering outlook, which he famously outlined in his influential book *The Uses of Literacy* (1958). However, the concentration on white, traditional working-class culture soon jarred with students steeped in the Vietnam era and Western imperialism, who rejected it as over-nostalgic and sentimental. Their experience of multi-ethnicity, patriarchy, American international cultural and military ascendancy and the power of television and the other branches of the mass media in popular culture forced teaching and research to adapt. Taking popular music seriously, examining the influence of television on popular consciousness, exploring the practices of mockery and disobedience at school as 'rituals of resistance', decoding soap operas, investigating fashion and language among youth subcultures as political statements, considering the racial overtones in aspects of policing and relating them to the economic crisis and tensions of inclusion at the heart of the British nation-state was heady, exhilarating stuff. For many, compared with the labours of orthodox students of English, forced to plough their way through *Beowulf* and Chaucer, and students enrolled on Sociology degrees, oppressively conscious of the twin imperatives of relating everything to the classical tradition of social theory or interrogating it against quantitative and qualitative methods of data collection, the Birmingham work seemed daring, relevant and bang up to date.

Gradually, especially after Hoggart left the Centre in 1968 to take up a position with UNESCO and Stuart Hall became Director, the main fronts of activity crystallized around issues of the mass media, state power, schooling, policing and race. In matters of data collection and the formulation of theory, Cultural Studies sought to be no less precise than the established disciplines. However, the relevance of research was ultimately defined as advancing the goal of political transformation in the direction of socialism. Under Hall's leadership, activities in the Centre became more theoretical and political. Between 1968 and 1979, among the topics studied were girls' magazines, youth subcultures, schooling, television, media representations of race, aspects of nationalism, women and the welfare state, the presentation of sport in the media, the emergence of rock music and discourses in TV comedy, mugging and policing. Significantly, new technologies of television and pop music, which widened access, were researched as having no less cultural value than stalwart technologies of writing, drawing and drama.

The main influence from the continental tradition was Marxism, especially the variations developed by Gramsci and the French social philosopher Louis Althusser. The Frankfurt School of cultural analysis was scarcely acknowledged. In part, this seems to have been the result of the non-availability of English language versions of the classic texts. However, it is also true that the reputation of the Frankfurt School was considered to be unduly pessimistic about the prospects of social change. Typically, it pitted questions of action and resistance against massive social, economic, political and cultural processes that expanded conformity and standardization. In contrast, the Birmingham approach was far more optimistic about turning the national-popular in the direction of progressive change.

A representative work of this period that exerted enormous influence was Stuart Hall's model of encoding and decoding. Originally published in 1973 and anthologized in Hall et al. (1980), the essay criticizes liberal models which treat the process of media communication as the mirror of social, political, economic and cultural reality. Against this, Hall submits that the media plays an active role in *assembling* a partial, patterned view of social reality. He coined the concept of *encoding* to refer to the process by which the media organizes information and communication as a text in order to achieve a preferred reading from viewers. Media professionals are central in the encoding process. It is their judgement of relevance and public interest that cooks raw social and political events and seeks to feed them to audiences. The process of reporting typically reinforces the position of the dominant interests in society so that this position is construed to be 'natural'. Encoding is not a closed system. On the contrary, once raw events have been cooked for the public, they are open to be consumed, rejected or disgorged by them. *Decoding* refers to the meanings that audiences bring to media presentations which challenge the meanings that are 'in dominance'. Hall (1980: 136) distinguishes three combinations in the cycle between encoding and decoding:

1   Dominant-hegemonic position   Here the decoding process in the audience complies with the encoded meanings invested in the communication process by media professionals and dominant social interests. In other words, the audience believes what it is told.
2   Negotiated position   This is the most common combination. It refers to the semi-acceptance or partial consumption of the encoded meaning supplied through the communication process. For example, audiences may accept the general legitimacy of the encoded representation of reality that is presented to them. At the same time, they may contrast this level of reality with the 'situational' knowledge of reality that derives from their experience of local culture and which may be quite dissonant with the generally legitimated level of reality.
3   Oppositional position   In this case, the audience accepts that raw events have been coded by the encoding process but elects to redefine the raw event through an alternative code.

It is fair to say that the Birmingham School had a colossal general 'demonstration effect' on how to do Cultural Studies. This was not so much because of any dirigiste tendency on the part of successive directors, but largely because it has been such an enormously fertile delta in easing the transition of key figures from the postgraduate level into important positions in the field. Consider the national and international Professoriat of Birmingham postgraduates who were either trained in Birmingham or have close associations with the Centre: Charlotte Brundson (University of Warwick); Hazel Carby (Yale University); Iain Chambers (Instituto Univeritario Orientale, Italy); John Clarke (Open University); Chas Critcher (Sheffield Hallam University); Linda Curti (Instituto Univeritario, Orientale, Italy); Michael Denning (Yale University); Paul Gilroy (London School of Economics); Larry Grossberg (University of North Carolina at Chapel Hill); Dick Hebdige (University of California at Santa Barbara); Mary Langan (Open University); Angela McRobbie (Goldsmiths College); David Morley (Goldsmiths College); Frank Mort (University of East London); Colin Sparks (University of Westminster); Chris Weedon (Cardiff University); Garry Whannel (University of Luton) and Paul Willis (University of Keele).

This is an extraordinarily gifted and influential collection of writers and researchers. It would be rash to maintain that they constitute a uniform group. On the contrary, there are many important differences between them. Nonetheless, they share common intellectual roots in Birmingham and have maintained the central values of their training in their research and writing. The main features of this outlook and approach are as follows:

1   *Politics* – a commitment to socialist change; a focus on the state as the main institutional lever of transformation; and an acute concern for the marginalized and the oppressed. This carries over into a respect for difference and a position on culture which situates questions of location, embodiment, emplacement and context in relation to power.
2   *Intellectual eclecticism* – although the roots of the Birmingham School were in the Marxist tradition, the obligation to roam far and wide in intellectual influences was recognized early on. This followed Gramsci's ideal of intellectual work based in the *organic intellectual*. That is, an intellectual labourer committed to keeping abreast of the latest ideas and transmitting them into popular culture. This passion for knowledge is prominent among the Birmingham circle and has resulted in an eclectic blend of theory from philosophy, sociology, literary criticism, political science and linguistics.
3   *Anti-essentialism* – the Birmingham commitment to locate culture in relations of power produced a strong reaction against essentialist

concepts. Instead, the *constructed, positioned* character of location, embodiment, emplacement and context are boldly stressed. This results in a textual approach to studying culture that focuses on the coding, theming and representation of identity, power and practice.

4 *Cultural populism* – the Birmingham tradition is strongly anti-elitist. It maintains that popular culture is worthy of study and that the representation of it by elite groups as marginal or insignificant is a question of cultural coding.

Birmingham was pivotal in the moment of the National-Popular in Cultural Studies. Stuart Hall emerged as an iconic figure, voracious in his reading, fertile in his thinking and vocabulary, politically committed and crossing boundaries of race, class and nation. The return of Larry Grossberg and the migration of Hazel Carby, Dick Hebdige and, for a time, Paul Gilroy to the United States disseminated many aspects of the Birmingham approach to North America. The superior funding condition of the USA ensured that by the mid-1990s America would be the dominant force in the academic division of labour in the field.

While the Birmingham tradition casts a long shadow over the approaches interested in cultural production and cultural politics, it would be a mistake to think of it as a one-man band. The work of Williams and Thompson preceded the Birmingham School and suggested different ways of doing Cultural Studies. In particular, Williams's interest in the media and cultural materialism influenced Nicholas Garnham (1992) and the *Media, Culture and Society* circle. They addressed questions of media power and manipulation in relation to democracy and citizenship.

At this moment, Cultural Studies was triangulated around communication, culture and politics in a pronounced way. The media, the state and class are privileged in building the horizon of cultural relations. Questions of globalization and hybridity were implicit, but did not figure significantly in analysis. True to its neo-Marxist roots, the national class struggle and the battle over state control and civil society was fundamental. At the same time, the discipline made a virtue of being eclectic in drawing on resources from linguistic philosophy, structuralism, phenomenology, social anthropology, mass communications research, literary theory and sociology. Politics of a particular kind was at the forefront of the National-Popular. Cultural Studies was theorized and practised as aligned to the goal of national-popular, *socialist* transformation.

The main challenge to the National-Popular moment in the 1980s was the rise of neo-liberalism. Thatcherism and Reaganism were founded on policies of trade union reform, market deregulation, tax cuts, strengthening policing and reducing expenditure on the welfare state. They promoted the resurgence of individualism in economy, culture, society and politics. Stuart Hall (1979) referred to this as 'the drift to the law and order society' and elsewhere (Hall 1989) coined the concept 'authoritarian populism' to refer to the new neo-liberal power bloc in the UK. By this term Hall meant a system of rule based on reducing public resources and promoting self-reliance which was – and this is what Hall and others believed was contradictory – funded upon the engineered consent of the working class, i.e. the people most adversely affected by the policies themselves. This was accomplished by a new economic rhetoric that stressed 'value for money', an 'audit culture' to check waste and the creation of a siege mentality against 'immigrants', 'aliens' and 'foreigners' in the national-popular. Thatcher introduced a new texture into this cultural fabric by referring to 'the enemy within', meaning protesters who resisted deregulation, the dismantling of the welfare state, privatization and other central planks of neo-liberal policy and thus implicitly threatened the whole way of life built around freedom. For his part, Reagan openly referred to the Soviet Union as 'an evil empire' and invested heavily in a 'Star Wars' technology designed to protect American interests. Upon the obvious collapse of communism in the mid-1980s, both Thatcher and Reagan presented themselves as global liberators, even though the main reason for disintegration was internal economic, political, religious and cultural contradictions in the Soviet system.

For Hall, authoritarian populism signified a dramatic shift in hegemony from the permissive society of the 1960s that had been the cradle of Cultural Studies. Neo-liberalism produced a crisis for the Left because it rejected the proposition that there is any credible alternative to market organization. Indeed, in the British press, Mrs Thatcher was colloquially known as *TINA* because of her indefatigable use of the phrase 'There Is No Alternative' in response to any criticism of neo-liberal doctrine and policies. The disintegration of communism in Eastern Europe appeared to reinforce the neo-liberal credo.

The Left faced a series of unexpected dilemmas. The West had won the Cold War. The Soviet system of communism was widely discredited, not least by Eastern European left-wing critics (Bahro 1978). There was no longer any system, however flawed, capable of mounting a tenable challenge to market capitalism. In addition, the political framework of resistance within the West had to be redefined away from the politics of class struggle to encompass related, but different forms of struggle having to do with gender, race, ethnicity, environmentalism, disability, anti-consumerism, globalization and a variety of other issues. This culminated in the revival of interest in questions of meaning, representation and multiple identity. These topics had already been addressed in many strands of continental philosophy and linguistics. As a result, Cultural Studies turned towards a more frontal engagement with these traditions and, in particular, sought to explore them in relation to cultural form and content.

An important tension during this period was between the 'malestream' of Cultural Studies and feminism (Women's Studies Group 1978). Women challenged the Marxist principle that property must be seen primarily in terms of class and economics. They submitted that in patriarchal culture (male dominated) the female body is treated as a type of property which is categorically different to class and economics. Further, this raises a separate set of cultural questions relating to the construction of gender and sexual identity, the language of male hegemony and representations of difference. McRobbie's (1978, 1991, 1996) work on representations of sexual difference in girls' comics suggested a new agenda for Cultural Studies. It can also now be read as one of the pioneering accounts of the significance of visual culture in Cultural Studies. Feminism unfastened the adherence of Cultural Studies to the Marxist tradition and introduced new questions of power, communication and representation. These became significant in the second moment of Cultural Studies.

Textual-Representational (1958–95)

In this moment the cultural role of the textual coding and theming of meaning became paramount. Mass culture is portrayed as an inherently *representational* world in which literary, visual and other narrative texts operate to order popular meaning. Initially, *semiotics* – the study of signs and sign cultures – promised to demystify this world. Barthes's collection of short essays on the creation of myth in popular culture, *Mythologies* (1957), was widely read and discussed. The most famous essay, which analysed a photograph from *Paris Match* of a black French soldier saluting what Barthes surmises is the *tricolore*, borrowed the distinction between *denotation* and *connotation* from structural linguistics. *Denotation* refers to the outward meaning that a text signifies. In the case of the photograph in question, the primary denotation is respect for the French nation. *Connotation* is a more complex concept, having to do with the chain of conscious and subconscious associations that relate to a given text. With respect to the photograph, Barthes maintains that what is connoted, among other things, is the fundamental benevolence of French colonialism. For Barthes, myth and ideology *naturalize* history to present the dominant power *regime* as inevitable, just and immoveable. At this time, the political role for Cultural Studies remains fairly conventional. As the *science* of signs, semiotics carries the promise of decoding the relationship between hierarchy, manipulation and order. The implication is that this type of rational knowledge will contribute to a better form of (socialist) society and culture.

However, during the 1970s, under the influence of post-structuralism, Lacanian psychoanalyis and the philosophy of deconstructionism, faith in semiotics as the science capable of yielding the true meaning of signs ebbed and eventually disappeared. This was connected with a massive retreat from the core values of order, rationality and progress. These values inspired the Enlightenment in the late eighteenth century and united the various progressive programmes of social and economic reconstruction and revolution associated with the liberal, conservative and socialist types of industrialization. By the late 1960s, critics of the Enlightenment contended that irrationality and unconscious forces are more powerful than reason and that rationality often has unacceptable consequences. These critics maintain that mass destruction, the attrition of the environment, the rise of totalitarianism and the Holocaust are the irrational consequences of forms of government organized around rational principles. Rationality unalloyed with emotions is therefore condemned as dehumanizing.

One aspect of this general retreat from the central values of the Enlightenment was to question the meaning of *all* signs. Barthes (1977) himself now argued that signs are *polysemic*. That is, they each have as many layers of meaning as the rings of an onion. Moreover, to shift the metaphor, these layers are not static. They change through practice and can be interpreted in various ways. Their meaning is a product of the *active involvement* of the reader, who brings to the task of interpretation a set of cultural competencies which frame meaning.

Since no ultimate meaning in sign systems is now acknowledged, the question of how cultural meaning occurs is redefined in terms of a range of questions concerning ambiguity, ambivalence and interplay. Volosinov's concept of multi-accentuality (1973) was enlisted to support the idea of the active reader, which was later expanded to 'the active audience'. Multi-accentuality highlights not only that signs carry plural meanings, but that these meanings are actively transformed by the context in which they are exchanged. The 'evaluative accent' or 'the grain of the voice', in Barthes's phrase (1992), in which a sign is expressed has the power to transform its meaning.

The thrust of these developments was to move Cultural Studies away from the task of demythologizing hierarchy and ideology. To be sure, demythologization remained part of the political agenda of emancipation. But it was now treated as secondary to examining the interplay and sliding of meaning and their relation to power. This was part of the task of building a new analytical perspective on meaning as, to use the term coined by Mikhail Bakhtin (1968), *dialogic*. This nicely combines the idea that meaning is the result of the active relationship between the speaker and the listener or the writer and the reader, and also that meaning changes through the development of dialogue. A dialogic approach maintains that the producer of an utterance does not hold a privileged position with respect to meaning. Recipients make meanings of utterance too. The result is a move away from an approach that views meaning as fixed or even necessarily hierarchical.

The emphasis on polysemy revitalized Saussure's proposition that meaning derives from the position of a sign in a given sign system, i.e. its relation to other signs. But now neither the sign nor the sign system are conceptualized as stable. This changed the nature of politics in Cultural Studies. It was no longer possible to envisage emancipatory practice in the conventional repertoire of neo-Marxist or Enlightenment goals, i.e. overturning the dominant authoritarian power regime and replacing it with a more egalitarian, democratic alternative, or to understand social change in terms of the struggle between central agents such as elites and masses, or classes. For the meaning of terms like 'egalitarian' and 'democratic' were no less subject to dialogic interpretation than 'power regime' and 'hierarchy'. The same applied to the concepts of 'elite', 'mass' and 'class'. The inevitable result of acknowledging the dialogic nature of meaning was the recognition of multiple modernities and the expansion of notions of variety and diversity with respect to politics.

In the first moment of Cultural Studies, politics was dominated by the neo-Marxist principle of class struggle. In the second moment, the multiplicity and diversity of politics came to the fore.

The representational character of the world was radically reaffirmed by the proposition that meaning is inherently textual and conditioned by the location of a term in a field of texts. This was known as *intertextuality* and the great influence it exerted in Cultural Studies at this time owed much to the work of the philosopher jacques Derrida. Derrida (1976) submits that no meaning exists outside of the system of signs. Because signs only have meanings in texts, it follows that our world and perceptions are inherently *textual*. Orthodox philosophers have contrasted nature with culture, as if the former precedes the latter. For Derrida this is faulty since nature is not prior, or external, to culture. On the contrary, it is nothing but the inscription of culture upon what is *represented* as Nature. *Inscription*, in the sense that we can only treat it as an object or have access to it through texts (sign systems), and texts are cultural products. In other words, Nature is now read as *culturally* defined and therefore culture is intrinsic to its meaning. This amounted to a dramatic rejection of the proposition that meanings are absolute, fixed, unified and beyond dispute. It invited you to re-evaluate culture as a relativistic universe in which meaning expressed knowledge and power. By extension it questioned all types of authority which are presented as 'ultimate' or 'final', since authority is redefined in relation to *intertextuality*. Hence, meaning is regarded as inherently mobile and therefore liable to change.

At first sight it may seem perverse to think that our world and perceptions are inherently textual. How can such an approach explain deeply personal experiences like falling in love or developing a passionate hobby? What has inscription to do with such things? The answer for those who espouse a textual-representational approach to the study of culture is a great deal. The act of falling in love is the choice of individual conscience. But what we understand as love is not simply physically dictated by our unique personal circumstances, desire and wants. It is culturally coded by the various cultural texts of romantic love, passionate attachment, companionship, love at first sight and so on. We can see this by briefly considering an example from comparative and historical analysis.

Robert Briffault's largely forgotten study of the troubadours in Medieval Europe (1965) skilfully reveals the role that poetry and music played in articulating a Romantic ideal of love in Court society. Briffault treats the troubadours not merely as artists, but as cultural and political agents. Their music, which speaks of the purity of love, everlasting bonds, the bliss of romance and the nobility of permanent union, added to the power of women in Court by defining them as the privileged handmaidens of romantic culture. Thus, women were associated with a representational code conveying a specific type of *power*, which was not only different from male power, but possessed the capacity to gear men into positions of dependency. This contrasted pointedly with the male world of arms and property.

Briffault's study shows how romantic love for the individual is born through cultural *inscription* – the representational and textual – the delicate calligraphy of music, poetry, ballads and other texts, which position people in relation to the emotional experience of romantic love *before* they enter into concrete relationships with one another. It is not that these texts can be said to create romantic love, nor that their existence deprives people of the consciousness of who and why to love. It is rather that our capacity to experience and understand romantic love is watermarked with their symbolism, narrative content and representation of textual yearning.

Derrida's concept of intertextuality has horizontal and vertical dimensions. The horizontal component refers to the position that one sign occupies in a field of texts. It can be examined in many areas, from how people differ on the introduction of parking restrictions in built-up zones or the value of the death penalty as a means of deterrence. These positions are often presented as alternatives. But by considering them from the perspective of intertextuality, they are shown to be interconnected and indeed, interdependent. One cannot argue against the death penalty unless a contrary set of arguments in favour of the punishment are in place. Horizontal meanings therefore imply that one meaning is bound up with others, even if these others are totally contrary and outwardly independent.

At first sight, the vertical component is more difficult to get your head around. According to Derrida the meaning of each sign is expressed through 'presence'. If I say that something is white I am attributing that meaning to the subject or pointing to an inherent property in it. In doing so I am *excluding* or *repressing* other meanings of colour. In Derrida's terminology, presence in language only works by rendering other meanings absent. Because he regarded language as always and already metaphorical, the distinction between presence and absence carries somewhat more than a purely technical meaning. Thus, the attribution of 'whiteness' to a culture excludes the contribution and represses the position of non-whites. So the distinction between presence and absence has strong implications for *political* understanding and practice. Meaning is never truly sovereign since it always contains *traces* of other meanings in the sign system and further is subject to change. The absent meanings may disrupt the sovereignty of a sign by announcing their presence in some way.

Derrida coined the term 'difference' to highlight that language always involves 'difference and deferral'. In the third moment of Cultural Studies, in which the postcolonial perspective on identity politics becomes paramount, the links between metaphor, exclusion and repression are elucidated in the context of exploring the question of empowerment. Derrida's work on language and power can be read as an important catalyst in this process.

In Cultural Studies the pairing of presence and absence exerted most influence over how cultural meaning is made. The idea that the *presence* of one meaning involves the *erasure* or *suppression* of other meanings was applied to a whole range of questions regarding the relationship between culture, identity and power. In the moment of the National-Popular, Cultural Studies was deeply concerned with the material level of culture. That is, the concrete effects of class inequality, regional distinctions, history and tradition. In the moment of the Textual-Representational, interest in the material level of culture was replaced with a major concern relating to how meaning is inscribed through texts and representations.

In Cultural Studies one of the leading examples of textual-representational analysis is Dick Hebdige's famous book *Subculture* (1979). A student in the Birmingham circle during its golden age, Hebdige was strongly influenced by continental theories of myth, discourse and differance. His study was a major publishing success attracting several generations of readers. It is not hard to fathom why. Where the majority of university courses in the social sciences of the day were becalmed in paddling through archival literature on relations in the largely decaying youth subcultures of teddy boys, skinheads, mods and rockers, it button-holed contemporary transformations in youth subcultures. Hebdige fixed his sights on the emerging Rasta and punk subcultures of the time in the UK, which were becoming more prominent in both national life and global culture through the mass media, and about which little had been written. He convincingly showed how youth subcultures employ irony and parody to create alternative spaces and identities in consumer culture. The book appeared to fulfil the promise of Cultural Studies by triumphantly providing an analysis of culture that was more *engaged* and *relevant* than traditional types of academic study. In addition, it was enriched with many arresting examples of how cultural theory might be used to decipher apparently meaningless forms of cultural practice.

Hebdige's book certainly gave the impression of having its finger on the cultural pulse. It addresses real contemporary, scene-changing, subcultural transformations and goes decisively beyond cultural appearances to illustrate how Cultural Studies might contribute to demystifying culture.

One of the book's most notable examples of how cultural styling operates and is resisted is Hebdige's application of *bricolage*. In the hands of the structural anthropologist Lévi-Strauss (1962), who coined the term, it refers to the process of relocating objects from one sign system to another so as to establish connections that would ordinarily be debarred by the rules of the 'home' sign system. Thus, he describes how the use of sorcery, superstition and myth among 'primitive' people is applied to make connections between signifying systems that are conventionally separated. Hebdige revitalizes the concept as a tool for making probing insights into contemporary culture. He shows how standard objects from consumer culture, such as Saville Row Edwardian jackets in Teddy Boy culture, co-opting Italian suits in mod culture and safety pins and bin liners in punk culture, were stripped of conventional associations of consumer culture and redefined as a parody of commodity fetishism. The latter is a term from Marxism that refers to the uncritical consumer worship of commodities. Undoubtedly, political *implications* are involved in Hebdige's analysis. However, his preoccupation is with the sheer invention and fertility of cultural styling by subcultures. He delights in showing how groups that are adversely positioned in relation to economic and political resources can nevertheless exert profound influence upon common culture through cultural styling.

Politics here is not so much concerned with achieving social and political transformation as recognizing the dynamics and legitimacy of difference. The emphasis is not on the domination of cultural signs or the mystification of the cultural sign economy. Rather, it is on active cultural styling and subcultural repositioning of styles and consumer commodities. That is, the use of cultural forms to convey an accent of 'alternative presence' or to articulate difference. The moment of the National-Popular carried with it the implication of transcendence. Theoretically, by unmasking cultural categories and power hierarchies, a qualitatively superior type of society and culture could be constructed. In the Textual-Representational moment transcendence ceases to be an issue in favour of an emphasis on the inexhaustible dynamics of cultural styling and the prolific and subtle inventiveness of cultural resistance. There is still a political dimension to this. Styling uses a variety of aesthetic and representational codes in a calculated attempt to achieve impact, to make people think about you in a particular way. Resistance is about rejecting the cultural definitions of the stylists and articulating identity. Hebdige was interested in how subcultures deliberately use coding and theming to achieve cultural impact. Theming, coding and representation are recognized as central ways in which the meaning of paramount reality is articulated and among the primary ways in which we position ourselves in relation to scarce economic, cultural, social and political resources to signify difference.

Globalization/Post-Essentialism (1980–)

Globalization means the dismantling of cultural, political, social and economic barriers via capital finance flows, mass migration and travel, the expansion of international information space through mass communication and the emergence of virtual technologies and associated cultures that challenge habitual notions of what seemed, until very recently, immoveable material barriers. It contradicts the orthodox wisdom about the nation-state by emphasizing the permeable character of national boundaries in a wired-up world. This alters the relation of Cultural Studies to the national-popular, since it implies that it is inadmissible to any longer confine questions of culture to national boundaries. *Bricolage* enters culture as a chronic feature of communication because cultural references are pitchforked from the national level to the global and available to anyone with an internet connection. This occurs through *disembedding*. By this term is meant the uprooting of cultural references from national-popular contexts and their relocation in the global arena.

Consider the ad campaign for Stella Artois in the summer of 2005. The company advertised the chance of winning a classic film on DVD and a trip to Alcatraz, San Francisco, for an exclusive screening of *The Birdman of Alcatraz* for anyone who bought a Stella over the summer. The advertisements consisted of a melange of fragmentary staged images on a high street in Scotland (a Scottish flag flies from the turret of a country house). A member of the paparazzi crosses the road in front of an abandoned VW Bug and a New York yellow cab while three men dressed in bowler hats, white overalls and boots sit at a table in front of a milk bar. In the background, a line of Minis is stacked up bumper to bumper. Two pool players walk on the pavement. A crashing bi-plane, a red balloon and falling frogs are dotted around the sky. A cloaked figure is crouched in a phone box making a call. A gunner with a sub-machine gun occupies the balcony of the town hall. A road sign in the background reads 'Arlington Road' in front of a pub called The Lion and the Unicorn and on the other side of the road there is a shoe shop called Steps, with a birdcage at the first floor window. There are massive cracks in the road and a hen or cockerel is marching due south east.

What is going on here? The images are of course, from the movies. The member of the paparazzi is a Weegee-like figure played by Joe Pesci in the film *The Public Eye* (1992). The yellow cab is a reference to

Scorsese's *Taxi Driver* (1976); the three figures in front of the milk bar are modelled on Alex and his droogs from Kubrick's *A Clockwork Orange* (1971); *Arlington Road* is also the name of Mark Pellington's film (1999) starring Jeff Bridges and Tim Robbins; the red balloon perhaps refers to Albert Lamorisse's film *Le Ballon rouge* (1956); the Scottish flag may be a reference to Mel Gibson's movie *Braveheart* (1995); the bi-plane which appears to be about to crash refers to Scorsese's *The Aviator* (2004); the mini-cars refer to the Mark Wahlberg film *The Italian Job* (2003) which was a remake of the original starring Michael Caine (1969); the birdcage on the first floor of the Steps store is a reference to *Birdman of Alcatraz* (1962) in which Burt Lancaster played Robert Stroud, the real life prisoner who became a world expert on birds and bird disease; the two pool players on the left of the advertisement are the characters played by Paul Newman and Tom Cruise in *The Color of Money* (1986); the figure making the call in the telephone box is *Superman*; the abandoned VW is perhaps meant to remind us of Herbie the Volkswagen Bug featured in *Herbie Rides Again* (1974) and *Herbie: Fully Loaded* (2005); Steps might be a reference to Hitchcock's famous adventure movie *The Thirty Nine Steps* (1935); the gunman may refer to the rebel schoolboy in Lindsay Anderson's *If . . .* (1968) or one of the terrorists in the *Die Hard* (1988, 1990, 1995) sequence starring Bruce Willis; the frogs falling from the sky are a reference to Paul Thomas Anderson's film *Magnolia* (1999); the cracks in the road signal natural disaster and are reminiscent of scenes in *Earthquake* (1974) starring Charlton Heston; the cockerel is one of the most famous brands used to advertise Pathé news reels in the cinema during the 1950s and 1960s, but the reference in the ad is probably to the film *Cidade de Deus* ('City of God', 2002) co-directed by Fernando Meirelles and Katia Lund; The Lion and the Unicorn is a reference to George Orwell's essay written in 1941 in London during war time bombing raids, which begins with the famous line: 'As I write, highly civilized human beings are flying overhead trying to kill me' (Orwell 1968: 74).

The advertisement illustrates how much multinational corporations have learned from Barthes and the Textual-Representational moment in Cultural Studies. The fragmentary film images operate through many chains of connotation. What is being connoted is not merely film references, but a definite lifestyle. Modern multinationals increasingly use adverts to position their commodities in particular lifestyles. In this case, Stella is aiming to reach more sophisticated drinkers, who have the knowledge and leisure to attend the cinema regularly, and use alcohol as part of a cultural experience that is self-defined as 'richer' than that of other social strata. Connecting with this lifestyle and combining it with Stella is all the more subtle and penetrating, because the advertisement operates largely on a subliminal level. You understand the chain of connotations only after reflection, and in making the relevant connections you have a sense of personal satisfaction that also works to affirm the value of the product and your identification with it.

The images used in the Stella advert show how signs in global culture are disembedded from their spatial and chronological positions to construct a global form of identity. The form of identity is based in recognition, the shared ability to decipher and demystify signs. It makes no appeal to tangible political unity or social solidarity. If it appeals to any identity type it is that of the savvy consumer, at home in a variety of cultural and spatial settings, whose capacity to decipher representational codes is a mark of individualism rather than identifying with the masses. Disembedding destabilizes ideas of fixed or unified identity because it enriches our understanding of variety, difference and movement.

The doctrine of essentialism holds that essence is prior to interpretation. For example, the essence of race, gender, class and so on is assigned *before* these things become objects for critical reflection and debate. In Christian thought they are literally God-given and in Muslim religion they are the word of the Prophet. Similarly, white racism submits that whites are essentially superior to non-whites and that the doctrine of racial equality is pure delusion.

The whole direction of Cultural Studies points in the opposite direction. In the moment of the National-Popular the idea of cultural essence was attacked by highlighting the place of power, especially class power, in constructing and imposing cultural meaning. In the moment of the Textual-Representational reality itself was portrayed as the articulation of texts and representations. Now, in the moment of Global/Post-Essentialism, the concept of 'multiple modernities' is elaborated and refined. The significance of intertextuality and discourse is reaffirmed and repositioned around a series of questions relating to identity.

Already, in the moment of the National-Popular, identity politics was gaining ground in Cultural Studies. Feminists raised the theme of masculine domination as a counterpoint to the stock emphasis on class (Women's Studies Group 1978). In addition, questions of race and ethnicity exposed the limitations of a rigid class-based approach to culture (Hall 1992). Now, under the influence of the writings of Derrida (1976) and especially Laclau and Mouffe (1985), a post-essentialist trajectory became ascendant. It denies any essential meaning to class, race, gender, nation and so on. Instead, it maintains that there is nothing outside discourse. Identity is no longer regarded as fate, although the relation between power and meaning is still observed. Identity, power and meaning are all understood and analysed as irretrievably implicated in discourse. Meanings are never fixed and always contradictory, since the presence of one meaning is always founded upon intertextuality and the absence of other meanings, which refuse to remain silent. However, presence is related to design, in the sense that there is a dimension of power behind them. Design may reflect the conscious interests of a particular group or social stratum or it may be the historical and social positioning of groups and strata that present their perspective of order and justice as 'natural' or 'inevitable'.

The proposition of fixed, exclusive identity in nationalism, culture, politics, personal life and everything else besides has been displaced by the proposition that identity is always and already hybrid and intrinsically mobile. At its simplest, hybridity means the mixing of cultural, ethnic and racial elements. As with intertextuality, it is useful to distinguish between vertical and horizontal dimensions to the concept. With respect to the horizontal dimension the development of globalization and the rise of multicultural society has exposed native cultures to new racial and cultural influences. Cultural mixing has occurred between native and migrant cultures. Western forms of diet, music, literature, dress, television, cultural values and much else have been revised in the process. World music, novels like *The Satanic Verses* by Salman Rushdie and *White Teeth* by Zadie Smith, the prose-poetry of Vikram Seth, movies like *My Beautiful Laundrette* (1985), *Dead Man* (1995), *Ghost Dog: The Way of the Samurai* (1999) and *Bend It Like Beckham* (2002) are direct cultural expressions of this process. But so are the rise of multicultural communities, the development of multi-ethnic cuisine, multicultural fashion style and transformations in the curriculum in schools and universities to reflect multicultural diversity and language patterns.

Turning now to the vertical dimension, multiculturalism and globalization have revealed that many Western traditions and values have exploited and developed non-Western precursors, often without giving them due recognition. Western science and medicine borrowed from China and India. These two countries were at the heart of what Pieterse (2004: 114) calls an 'Afro-Eurasian' imperial world economy which predates the nineteenth-century Western model by several centuries. This way of thinking exploits and develops Derrida's notion that presence always involves absence. It implies that we should abandon essentialist ideas of identity and replace them with what is sometimes called 'hyphenated-identity'. So the old ideas of British, American or Australian citizen become redefined in terms of Black-Heteronormative-British, Indian-Gay-American or Australian-Greek-Disabled, and so on. Identity therefore is always conceptualized as hybrid and sliding.

In the National-Popular moment, Gramscian's were critical of the 'culturalist' tradition in British Cultural Studies exemplified by the thought of Hoggart, Thompson and Williams. The reason was that it was deemed to be too culturally insular in that it fixed cultural studies in the examination of national-popular culture (Hall 1980). In the Representational-Textual moment, the move to picture meaning in terms of intertextuality and create a dialogic approach to culture prepared the ground for post-essentialist thinking, for it uprooted old ideas of cultural hierarchy and exclusivity. In the most radical versions of the Globalization/Post-Essentialist moment, *all* meaning is regarded as prone to slippage, and nothing is recognized outside discourse. The focus of political action in the moment of Globalization/Post-Essentialism is on disrupting the logic of capitalism and exposing the limits of fixed identity thinking.

A variety of social movements have developed around these responses. These have many different political, economic, social and political goals. But they all express a distinctive *Weltanschauung*, or 'spirit of the times', that recognizes that power positions identity. By extension, they recognize pivotal critical design in challenging the cultural allocation of identity by revealing the powers that assign difference or exposing the marginalization and repression that the affirmation of identity produces. For example, consider the Adbusters Media Foundation, a prominent anti-consumerist group. It's Web Manifesto declares:

> We are a global network of artists, activists, writers,
> pranksters, students, educators and entrepreneurs.
> We are downshifters, shit-disturbers, rabble-rousers,
> incorrigibles and malcontents. We are anarchists,
> guerrilla tacticians, neo-Luddites, pranksters, poets,
> philosophers and punks. Our aim is to topple existing
> power structures and forge a major shift in the way we
> will live in the 21st century. We will change the way
> information flows, the way institutions wield power, the
> way food, fashion, car and culture industries set their
> agendas. Above all, we will change the way we interact
> with the mass media and we will reclaim the way
> in which meaning is produced in our society.
> (www. adbusters.org)

This is an explicitly *cultural* programme of political action aimed at dismantling dominant structures of meaning by disrupting mass communications and the logic of consumer culture. It is also dedicated to illuminating how identity is positioned and polished in consumer culture. Among the practical methods used in pursuit of these ends are culture-jamming, pastiche and cyber-squatting. The object is to reclaim the 'mental environment' from the influence of multinationals and the corporatist state (a form of state which is dedicated to preserving and expanding capitalist society). No coherent politics of transcendence is offered. The Adbusters group is about unravelling power in consumer culture rather than outlining or implementing a coherent alternative. In so far as emancipatory potential is recognized, it lies in encouraging people to confront and understand how forms of identity are located in consumer culture by multinationals and the corporatist state. This knowledge may be shared, but it does not necessarily result in the recognition of collective identity whether it takes the form of a class, a race, a gender or some other political, economic, cultural and social category. Rather, West's 3 D's (deconstruction, demythologization, demystification) (1992) are powerfully reaffirmed.

The work of Edward Said (1978, 1993) suggests yet another way of how the Globalization/Post-Essentialist moment has developed in Cultural Studies. His concern with culture decisively shifts the question of studying culture from the national to the national-global level. It also seeks to displace models of cultural superiority and subordination with a more morally diffuse and culturally complex approach that stresses the interpenetration of cultures. It begins by asking how is it possible to recognize and practise culture from a point of oblivion? This sounds like a conundrum. Yet it is the position that Said attributes to Palestinians in 1948, following the construction of the state of Israel. How to act when you have been administratively erased? From the outset, Said's approach seeks to treat cultures as interpenetrating, intertwined processes. So he also asks, what are the means of maintaining authority in a democracy after you have acted as the agent of erasure? These questions were among Said's first response to the Arab–Israeli war of 1967.

To answer these questions, Said sought not the paths of international relations and political science, although these disciplines are certainly recognized by him as influencing his outlook. Instead, he set himself an aesthetic and historical task: to trace the vast contours and obscure tectonics of the Western cultural representation of the Orient. It is upon the rules, exclusions and prohibitions maintained by this system that the place of the Orient and that which pertains to it are positioned. The geo-political elimination of Palestine is a concrete case of this positioning in operation.

Said (1978, 1993) calls this system of representation *Orientalism*. As a collective noun it bundles together a variety of Western political, scientific, social, literary, aesthetic and poetic *discourses*, their representation and interpenetration with one another and, finally, their inscription upon culture, politics and nature. According to Said, under colonialism the field of white power devised and elaborated the discourse of Orientalism to treat non-white culture as symbolically and practically extraneous to white culture. Yet the very categories it uses are complementary and interdependent instead of isolated or detached. There are strong echoes here of Foucault's argument that discourse is fundamental in organizing identity and Derrida's proposition that presence always involves absence.

As an example of how identity operates through splitting, bracketing and erasure, Said (1993) takes a work of high culture that outwardly is unconnected with questions of colonial politics: Jane Austen's *Mansfield Park*. In the novel, the wealth of the English estate is founded upon the productivity of the Caribbean plantation owned by the Bertram family. Austen's discussion of power and position in Mansfield Park is rich and penetrating while her treatment of conditions in the Antigua plantation are seldom more than summary. The colony is bracketed out from the main action, the decisive presence in the novel, which is the comings and goings of English aristocratic society. Yet in the narrative the viability of life in Mansfield Park clearly relies upon the plantation turning a profit. The absence of the Antigua plantation in Austen's novel cannot disguise its fundamental presence in everything that happens in Mansfield Park.

What is true for the novel is true of all aspects of Orientalism. For Said, cultures are not watertight containers. On the contrary they are porous, absorbing many 'foreign' influences even while insisting upon their formal independence and integrity. Through a *contrapuntal* reading of culture, that is an approach which counterposes subordination with domination and absence with presence, it is possible to reveal hybridity and that the formal hierarchy of power has feet of clay. Certainly, for Said, the point of studying Orientalism is not to be subject to its discipline, but to *resist*.

Governmentality/Policy (1985–)

The key intellectual influence here is Michel Foucault. His work on history and discourse twinned culture with representation (Foucault 1977, 1979). It connected questions of representation with political institutions, forms of social life and systems of prohibitions and constraints. At first sight, this places him in the textual-representational camp. But Foucault's work is distinct in systematically relating questions of culture and representation to history, power, knowledge, problems of social justice and government. Foucault saw himself as a historian tracing what he called the *genealogy* of knowledge and power and their effects in producing truth. Genealogy here means the system of representations and ideals that creates versions of culture and promotes them as true. What emerges most powerfully from this approach is the 'constructed', 'positioned' character of culture. In Cultural Studies this translates into an interest in how power and knowledge are applied to govern culture (Bennett 1998). In particular, Foucault's notion that identity and practice are organized through *discourse* has been widely adopted and developed.

For Foucault, discourse refers to a particular combination of knowledge and power. Representations of this combination shape cultural identity and practice. The most famous example from Foucault's writings (1979) is sex. According to Foucault, the category of sex is far from naturally given. Rather it is part of what he calls a 'regulatory practice' that arranges and controls the bodies it governs. Historically speaking, the various discourses about sex – the knowledge and power imparted about physical attraction, cultural allure, sexually transmitted disease, the sexual characteristics of different races, infant sexuality, sexual abnormality and so on – construct our sexual identity. These discourses do not *determine* sexual identity. Yet it is impossible to communicate sexually or to take sexuality as an object of study without observing their parameters.

In Cultural Studies the interest in how practice is shaped by discourse has crystallized in problems of governmentality and power (O. Bennett 2001; T. Bennett 1998; Meredyth and Minson 2001; Mercer 2002). The writings of American-based authors such as Stanley Aronowitz, Michael Curtin and Doug Kellner provided an important theoretical input which both utilized and reacted against Foucault's work.

The general problematic informing all of this work is the role of culture in shaping identity and practice. Among the topics investigated are how public funds are used to preserve heritage; the ways in which community values are promoted through culture; how investment in culture advances nationalism; and how branding represents identity. This work is often antagonistic to critical theories of culture on the grounds that Cultural Studies is not only about theory but also about the direct government of culture. Bennett (1992) proposed that education and research in Cultural Studies should be oriented to producing 'technicians' to practically manage culture. It is not clear if the dichotomy between technicians and critical theorists is quite so stark. Many a technician is concerned not only with managing culture but with realizing a personally felt version of 'the imaginary'; just as in proposing alternatives to cultural form and practice, critical theorists raise many practical and technical questions (McGuigan 2004: 15).

An important question in this moment is the freedom of the public to challenge and resist the cultural genres and systems of cultural production generated by the state and private business conglomerates that seek to position the citizen and consumer in culture. McGuigan's elaboration and revitalization of Habermas's concept of 'the public sphere' (1962) has been especially important in this regard (McGuigan 1996, 2004). The role of the public in modifying the behaviour of the powerful is not infallible, but, historically speaking, it has become culturally significant. It is the result of the historical emergence of the public sphere. *The public sphere* might be defined as the real and ideal space in society in which executive and legislative authority is exchanged, developed, criticized and elaborated through real and ideal models of open discussion. Habermas (1962) uses the concept mainly to examine how rational and political space opened up in the eighteenth century to produce the basis of today's citizenship rights, entitlements, pressure groups and parliamentary democracy. He also distinguishes *the literary public sphere*, which is the space of philosophy, journalism, literature and belles-lettres in which cultural questions of how to live, the greater good, moral precept and ethical duty are aired and cultivated. Several commentators now argue that the concept needs to be radically revised to embrace cultural and global dimensions. That is, the literary public sphere has expanded in response to the energy of popular culture at large. Its dimensions are now international (Garnham 1992; McGuigan 2000).

Of course, there are many qualifications that need to be added to these bald propositions. Anglophone regions do not necessarily translate into *uniform* anglophone cultures. Just because *The Sopranos* is watched regularly in Manchester, Melbourne and Milwaukee doesn't mean that we can infer cultural unity thereto; any more than the vast global audience for the funeral of Princess Diana in 1997 can be taken as evidence of a 'one-world' position with respect to the meaning of her life and its relation to the British royal family. Global events are inflected and scrambled by local conditions. The same item of global news carries a different cultural payload in Adelaide, Auckland, Akron and Amsterdam. Nonetheless, there is a palpable sense in which the global satellite media positions all of these places on the same playing field, in which a common agenda of issues and opinions is shared.

Because of this, there is considerable public disquiet about the concentration of media power in a handful of multinational conglomerates. Might follows the authority to shape people's opinions of cultural, economic, political and social reality. To this extent, it is perfectly reasonable to contend that media moguls like Rupert Murdoch, who controls News Corporation, possess undue and even dangerous power to influence public opinion. Why else do political leaders of all parties seek to cultivate close relationships with Murdoch and his media lieutenants?

At the same time it is also true that the connectivity of the public to global news and opinions has never been greater. Citizenship in modern culture is only effective through *information* and the scale of the global media means that as an ordinary part of daily life individuals are exposed to unprecedented data streams. Nor can these streams be blandly regarded as universally subject to multinational manipulation. The technology of contemporary culture offers channels of resistance and opposition.

The internet is a key resource for exchanging and developing data. It cannot be effectively policed and it permits historically unparalleled levels of news exchange and civic debate. When four suicide bombers attacked the London underground and public bus system in July 2005, I was in Stockholm. Within minutes I was texted with the news by people in the UK. I followed media reports live on my mobile phone web service. Throughout the day I engaged in web-reports, texting and e-mail exchange about the extent of the tragedy and the identities of the bombers. News isn't just fast, it is instantaneous, and it isn't confined by national boundaries or the representations of multinational corporations and the state. It is global and popular (McGuigan 1992).

Politically speaking, the global public sphere is a significant, real and ideal counterweight to the abuse of power and the violation of human rights. For example, media coverage of and public reaction regarding the photographs showing maltreatment by American military personnel of Iraqi prisoners held in the Abu Ghraib military base produced worldwide condemnation. Seven military police guards were eventually court-marshalled. The incident confirmed widespread fears throughout the world about the nature and intent of American foreign policy in Iraq. It changed the culture of Allied occupation by strengthening standards of transparency and the protection of human rights.

The moment of Governmentality/Policy acknowledges the role of culture in attracting investment and promoting social integration. Cultural investment correlates positively with quality of life issues and this, in turn, attracts economic investment. Workers don't simply want good jobs, they want to live in a nice place (Mercer 2002). This logic has been an important factor in municipal policies of regeneration. Investment in cultural resources has increased the appeal of cities like Glasgow, Manchester, Birmingham and Sheffield in the UK as sources for industrial relocation. Similarly, the economist Richard Florida (2002) has famously argued that the buoyancy of economies in San Francisco, San Diego, Austin, Boston and Seattle in the 1990s owed much to city strategies of planned cultural investment.

What emerges most unequivocally from this literature is the increasing importance of culture as an economic resource. In the UK, the Department for Culture, Media and Sport has specifically identified cultural institutions as tools for social engineering (DCMS 2000). The ends of social engineering are usually defined in general terms as empowerment, social inclusion and distributive justice. While few would dispute the value of these ends, the devil is in the detail. Questions of governmentality and policy involve large and difficult arguments over cultural values and positive discrimination. An emerging theme in this position is how resource allocation can function equitably through a politics of difference. In particular, it refers to how individuals and groups exploit cultures of inclusion and positive discrimination to position themselves more favourably in relation to economic, cultural and political scarcity. This is proving to be a useful corrective to relativist and post-identity arguments in Cultural Studies. It demonstrates that for many individuals and groups, especially those located at the margins of social, economic and political inclusion, identity politics remains a basic issue of culture.

These then, are what I take to be the four moments of Cultural Studies since its academic inception, just over forty years ago. The approach you chose will have much to do with what 'naturally' makes sense to you. Except that one of the pleasures of Cultural Studies is that it reveals that the 'natural' attachment you have to a particular method or theory often turns out to reflect subconscious aspects of your personality, cultural background and time. We are all culturally organized and positioned. The study of this process should help us to gain distance from 'native' views of society, culture and politics. By standing outside yourself and the cultural attachments in which you are emplaced and located as a condition of birth, you have the chance to formulate a wider, more objective perspective about identity, practice and politics. In any case, your approach to Cultural Studies is likely to draw on elements from all four moments.

Cultural Studies at the crossroads

The transitions between the four moments reflect practical efforts to understand the course of postwar history, culture and society. Arguably, since 1979, the defining feature in the development of all four moments has been internationalization. The Birmingham Centre was instrumental in this trend. The migration of Birmingham alumni spread the word in other countries and, in doing so, exposed the limitations of the British approach. In particular, the British insistence on the centrality of class did not translate well into settings where traditions of religious division, racial conflict, ethnic enmity and colonial friction were deeply embedded. In addition, partly in response to the collapse of communism in Eastern Europe, and *glasnost* (open consultative government and wider dissemination of information) and *perestroika* (the reform of the centrist system of government in the Soviet Union, first proposed by Leonid Brezhnev in 1979 and actively pursued by Mikhail Gorbachev from 1985), continental philosophy placed a revised emphasis on the construction and deconstruction of cultural meaning, the centrality of discourse and the micro-politics of power. These developments combined to weaken the old emphasis in the Left upon class solidarity and class struggle. Instead the emphasis switched to multiple divisions in society and culture with questions of difference, inclusion and exclusion occupying centre stage.

At the same time, the expansion of satellite broadcasting and the rise of the internet accentuated the significance of the media and mass communication in everyday life. It was no longer satisfactory to confine questions of coding and representation to the territory of the nation-state, since mass communications and global capitalism refused to recognize the integrity of these boundaries. In addition, academics themselves became more mobile, participating in international conferences and, as the internet matured, developing stronger relationships with colleagues living thousands of miles away than with members of the same department housed in the same corridor. The disembedded scholar, at home in Europe, Australia and the United States, with friendship networks and peer-reviewed publications in all three continents, became much less of a rarity. A figure, like the moral philosopher Peter Singer, could be educated in Melbourne and Oxford, get his first job as a lecturer in Oxford, move back to Melbourne to hold posts at La Trobe and Monash, migrate to become Professor of Bioethics at Princeton University in 1999, accept a joint part-time appointment in the University of Melbourne in 2005, while lecturing throughout in Europe, Australia and North America. Not all academics could achieve this cosmopolitan existence, an existence in which the individual feels at home in many different urban-industrial settings. But after the 1980s cosmopolitanism replaced regionalism and nationalism as the ideal ethos of most of the leading figures in the Humanities and Social Sciences.

One sign of the growing significance of internationalization and cosmopolitanism was the establishment of The 'Crossroads' International Conference in Cultural Studies, in Tampere, Finland in 1996. Its mission statement acknowledged the significance of difference, hybridity and mobility in Cultural Studies:

> Cultural studies is not a one-way street between the centre
> and peripheries. Rather, it is a crossroads, a meeting point
> in between different centres and intellectual movements.
> People in many countries and with different backgrounds
> have worked their way to the crossroads independently. They
> have made contacts, exchanged views and gained inspiration
> from each other in pursuing their goals. The vitality of
> cultural studies depends on a continuous traffic through
> this crossroads. Therefore the conference organizers invite
> people with different geographical, disciplinary and theoretical
> backgrounds together to share their ideas. We encourage
> international participation from a wide range of research
> areas. (http://culstud.org/crossroads/whatis.htm)

The 'Crossroads' conference takes place every two years and is regarded as a key switchboard for new debates and ideas.

Bound up with this crystallization of the field was a subtle reconfiguration of the position of politics in Cultural Studies. For most of the time during the moments of the National-Popular and in the first decade or so of the Textual-Representational class struggle was regarded as central. As the 1970s unfolded, the influence of feminism and racial difference complicated this picture. Cultural Studies retained a commitment to socialist change, but it was no longer exclusively or even primarily pursued through an interest in class politics. With the internationalization of the discipline, political issues have fanned out to cover sexuality, gender, embodiment, the environment, new ethnicities, colonialism and postcolonialism as well as class, gender and race.

Students of Cultural Studies sometimes find it tricky to extract a coherent political programme from these inputs. Perhaps the best way to think of it is to submit that Cultural Studies has redoubled its commitment to the politics of emancipation. However, it has shifted from examining class as a master identity to wider questions of the dynamics of identity. The multiple, many-sided ways in which nurturing in culture fixes identity, elicits resistance and promotes change form the core of Cultural Studies today. The focus now is upon identity politics and social movements.

6

Situating Yourself in Culture

Is there a methodology that might help us to situate ourselves in culture more objectively and assist in the selection of the right approach for the right set of questions? Now, a variety of specialized qualitative and quantitative methods exist. They have their uses in investigating cultural relations. But there is a sense in which everyone is a cultural methodologist long *before* approaching specialized methodologies of cultural investigation.

Before birth, we are culturally positioned. Our practical approaches to cultural life are also coded and themed by our cultural circumstances, even though we may depart from them in many particulars of individual conscience and taste as our life experience expands. At a basic level, our positioning equips us with characteristic ways of understanding and deciphering the cultural world. It follows that we cannot operate successfully in culture without being skilled experts in cultural methodology. Of course we don't call it this. We call it our 'natural' way of relating to the world. Far from being 'natural', it is culturally conditioned.

Culture is a complex and multi-layered phenomenon. How can we gain a perspective on our 'natural' way of reading the cultural world and find a basis for comparing and contrasting it with other cultural viewpoints? We must begin with the individual's perspective on cultural genre, production, consumption and politics. But this is unlikely to yield useful analytic data, unless we recognize the *situated* character of the individual, and take steps to unravel the nature of this condition.

Fig. 6.1   The pattern of cultural relationships

We can engage in cultural mapping in a basic way by analysing the pattern of cultural relations in terms of four references points: embodiment, emplacement, location and context (see figure 6.1). What is meant by these terms?

Location

Let's start with location, because that is where culture is directly *made* as individuals interact, help, represent, struggle, conflict and co-operate with each other, in relation to scarce economic, social, political and cultural resources. It is the *sensuous, active* form of cultural practice. Obviously, at the most basic level this refers to physical presence and interaction, i.e. individuals in practical involvement with others. As such, all of us might be said to be on a default setting to apply and decipher culture. For how can we conduct our lives without exploiting, interpreting and developing cultural resources? When you wake, wash, comb your hair and brush your teeth in the morning you are following cultural codes. When you go to the cinema to see a movie you are observing culturally themed patterns of behaviour. So is everything culture?

Not quite. Material reality exists outside culture: a rose is a rose is a rose. But culture provides the only way of accessing this reality, communicating it with others and formulating perspectives upon it. If this is the case, culture might reasonably be said to be *implicit* in everything. Studying how it is implicated helps us clarify general and local patterns of behaviour and predict paths of development.

The most obvious setting to explore location is through *on-location* behaviour. By this is meant the interaction between people in definable cultural settings. Among the settings in which students of cultural behaviour have investigated on-location practices and forms are schools, workplaces, clubs and pubs. The list is potentially infinite. Any cultural setting that engages individuals in culturally patterned sequences of interaction qualifies. We might make a distinction between formal and informal codes of patterning. Formal codes refer to what might be called the *house rules* of location. Institutions like schools, hospitals and workplaces have written rules of conduct. Although they are compatible with a degree of latitude in how people actually behave, they also discipline behaviour and curtail conduct that is challenged as *infractious* or 'rule-breaking'. But of course, through the process of growing up in families, communities, social classes and ethnic groups, individuals develop informal rules of practice and ways of seeing the world that also pattern behaviour on-location. The French sociologist of culture Pierre Bourdieu (1984) calls these rules and orientations to the world *habitus* and submits that they are fundamental in understanding cultural practice. By observing formal and informal patterns, or participating in them, we gain insights into how cultural resources are distributed, genres of cultural behaviour are reproduced, the ways in which cultural order is sustained, and the power relations behind cultural form and content.

Because culture is implicit in all patterns of human behaviour, studying location cannot be confined to face-to-face interaction. For the trajectory of this interaction is influenced by cultural symbols, motifs and myths that are also integral to on-location practice. For example, you may be interested in studying behaviour in a celebrity fan club. Fans bring their own cultural baggage to the fan club, i.e. their personal knowledge, desires, fantasies, wants and cravings. But this baggage is assembled through the relationship between the individual and the *public face* of the celebrity (Rojek 2001). That is, the *representation* of celebrity produced by the media. Since fans seldom meet celebrities, let alone form friendships with them, they rely on the representations produced in magazines like *Heat, Closer* and *Hello* in the UK and, in the USA, *People, In Touch* and *Star*; the celebrity gossip columns of tabloid newspapers; celebrity bulletin boards; the news; biographies; and television and radio interviews. These are often explicitly voyeuristic, encouraging fans to enter the private lives of celebrities albeit on the terms set by the conventions of the celebrity media. Interestingly, they have recently been supplemented by the emergence of a plethora of celebrity gossip blogging sites, such as <www.hollywooddrag.com>, <www.celebrity-scum.com> and <www.Defamer.com>. It is estimated that these sites outnumber celebrity magazines by 150 to 1 (*Baltimore Sun* 12.08.05). Why this is noteworthy is because it indicates the strength of consumer activism in following celebrity culture. In contemporary, media-dominated culture, celebrities are enormous sources of gossip, role models, fantasy and voyeurism. While this says something about the power of the media today, it also reveals a good deal about what might be called *the inspiration deficit* in contemporary life, as millions of people appear to want to be 'filled' with the lives of the famous and the glamorous. But this is perhaps the subject for another book!

As we have already noted, Stuart Hall et al. (1980) argued that the media does not reflect reality, it *codes* it. This is certainly true of celebrity culture. The interaction of fans on-location in fan clubs is the expression of various intersecting codes of representation and associated initiatives of decoding. In other words, the genre of celebrity culture as it is expressed in fan clubs can be studied as a type of location. It positions the celebrity before us in a specific network of meanings, which inform face-to-face interaction. Moreover, as with all types of on-location behaviour there is a politics attached to participating in cultural genres.

A particularly interesting point in which genres can be investigated is when the various intersecting codes of representation are publicly violated. The trial of Michael Jackson on child molestation charges in 2005 provides a rich and well-documented example. Jackson's trial was a global media event, some might say a global media circus. It illustrates very well, not only how celebrities are coded and decoded in popular culture, but also how some forms of high profile on-location behaviour are now routinely disembedded from their local contexts and subjected to multiple interpretation through globalization. During the weeks of the trial, it is difficult to believe that anyone with a television set, web link or radio could have avoided reports of the exchanges between the prosecution and defence and news of Jackson's reaction to them. His apparent gathering anxiety and physical frailty were prominent themes in media reports.

The trial concluded by finding Jackson not guilty on all counts. However, culturally speaking, the acquittal was far from amounting to a public vindication. The public face of Michael Jackson was tarnished with insalubrious details about his private life. His fitness to be with children was questioned. The police confiscated pornographic material from his Neverland retreat in California. His precarious finances were laid bare before the public, and invited widespread charges of irresponsibility and reckless, vulgar, conspicuous consumption. *Billboard* magazine polled 6,851 readers during the final week of the trial and found that 46 per cent believed that Jackson's career as a superstar was finished. Only a quarter believed that he could put the scandal of the charges of child molestation behind him (*The Times* 09.06.05).

Doubtless, many of Jackson's fans will stay loyal. After all, in the 1980s Jackson's album *Thriller* sold 59 million copies, a figure that qualifies it for the accolade of the bestselling record in history. Jackson's music, and his public image, was internalized by a huge number of fans as a key reference point in the construction of their self-image and formation of identity. As a role model they looked to him for inspiration and trust. It is exactly the issue of trust that has been most damaged by the charges of child abuse. The accusation of exploiting the trust of the most vulnerable in our society has turned the whole question of Jackson's moral character and sincerity into a public issue. We know from Michael Billig's study (1992) of how the British public identifies with the culture of the royal family that many ordinary people relate to the birth, death and scandals of royalty as scripts of instruction, or markers for events in their lives. In advanced celebrity culture, with its ever-changing stratosphere of charismatic stars and celebration of conspicuous consumption and leisure, the interface of co-existence between fans and celebrities is extensive. Identification is orchestrated and recognized at many points. The lives of celebrities provide parables of instruction for fans and general audiences. Hence, many women throughout the world identified with the marital travails of Princess Diana, so much so that a cult of what might be called 'damaged celebrity' developed around her, even before she died. The battles of Elizabeth Taylor, Anthony Hopkins and Robbie Williams with alcohol; the struggles of Robert Downey Junior, Keith Richards, Charlie Sheen, Kiefer Sutherland, Carrie Fisher, Whitney Houston, Kate Moss and Pete Doherty with drugs; the bouts of depression suffered by Ted Turner, Alanis Morissette, Jean-Claude Van Damme, Drew Barrymore, Tipper Gore and Kurt Cobain; the public accounts of post-natal depression made by Courteney Cox, Brooke Shields, Natasha Hamilton (Atomic Kitten) and Elle Macpherson; and the confessions of eating disorders made by Jane Fonda, Mary-Kate Olsen and Justine Bateman – all may be interpreted as an extension of a form of public therapy culture in which ordinary men and women are encouraged to make sense of problems and difficulties in their own lives by identifying with the experience of stars.

Michael Jackson provided millions of people with the soundtrack for their youth and a positive role model. It is reasonable to assume that many of his fans have sympathy with his emotional difficulties in respect of fame and the paparazzi. Nonetheless, the stigma that surrounds charges of child molestation is hard to live down. In Britain the 1999 conviction of the 1970s' pop idol Gary Glitter on charges of child pornography and the prison sentence that the pop producer, media mogul and TV presenter Jonathan King received in 2001 after being found guilty of child abuse charges wrecked their careers.

Jackson was acquitted of all charges. But the last fifteen years of his career have been dogged by unsavoury rumours concerning his relationships with children. His popularity has been badly dented. This is reflected in his recent album sales. *Blood on the Dance Floor* (6 million) and *Invincible* (8 million) are a long way from the triumphs of his post-*Thriller* releases, *Bad* (28 million) and *Dangerous* (29 million). The public airing of child abuse allegations during his trial will probably persuade many of his fans that there is no smoke without fire. However, unjust this might be – and to repeat, Jackson was acquitted – it will be challenging to overcome.

Cultural Studies invites you to view reality as multiply coded. The public world of news and information is themed by the media, the state and multinational companies. Individuals bring to the public world the classificatory schemes and ultimate values that we internalize through membership of our families, schools and communities.

Pierre Bourdieu's term *habitus* (1984) refers to the generative principles that produce and reproduce the practices of a cultural formation. By the term 'generative principles' is meant the codes, classificatory frameworks and traditions that define a particular culture. These principles are evident in all forms of cultural interaction, but they are not equivalent for all cultural groups. *Difference* and *power* are offered as foundational principles of culture and politics. Because they are positioned in relation to various types of access to scarce resources, difference and power involve *struggle*. This is why Cultural Studies pictures culture as the intersection of force and resistance.

The aftermath of Michael Jackson's trial positions him differently in culture. It also situates his fans in a radically revised relationship to his public face. What he and the cultural genre surrounding him denote and connote has changed. His management team will doubtless be eager to restore the hegemonic code of the 1980s that presented him as a desired, dynamic performer and one of the greatest pop superstars in the history of popular music. But this now requires extensive negotiation with critical and carping elements in the media that continue to generate a rumour mill of hearsay about his private life, and sections of his fan base that may have now concluded that there is no smoke without fire.

Jackson's infamous TV interview with Martin Bashir, *Living With Michael Jackson* (2003), was an attempt to present the real Michael Jackson to viewers. The image of the singer's obvious eccentricity and views on sleeping with children are widely regarded to have been a catalyst in the decision of the police to bring charges of child molestation. So another attempt at an interview based in candour and sincerity or a documentary may backfire unless it is carefully orchestrated by the Jackson camp. Yet a cosmetic account of the issues that precipitated the trial will probably be counter-productive. Portraying Jackson as a helpless victim begs the question of why others have presented him as a sexual predator and is likely to stir up more demons than it lays to rest.

A more compelling strategy might be to return to recording and public performance with the aim of crushing the rumour mill by the sheer force of his artistry. This has the advantage of disarming his critics by letting his music do the talking. However, if this were attempted it would be in the context of a recent history of disappointing record sales and it would carry the risk of public protests during his performances. It is a tricky moment in Jackson's career. It will be interesting to see how he handles the re-positioning of his public face and, in particular, if he can discard the barnacles of discredit, rumour and hearsay that are now attached to him. Similarly, it will be fascinating to see how his fans redefine his public face in the light of the charges made against him and the troubling rumours that surround him.

Frank Sinatra experienced a similar episode of falling and descent in the late 1940s and early 1950s as a series of media accusations concerning involvement with the Mafia, sympathies for communism, promiscuity and violence mounted up against him. It took seven years for him to regain his popularity, which he accomplished by winning an Oscar for his performance in the film *From Here To Eternity* (1953) and launching a series of classic album recordings for Capitol Records (Rojek 2004). But Jackson faces a bigger struggle because paedophilia is such a widely detested condition in popular culture and the legal attribution of it to him is correspondingly harder to live down, despite his exoneration from the charges in the court.

Questions of location have been explored in various ways in Cultural Studies. Paul Willis's study *Learning to Labour* (1977), which is widely regarded as a contemporary classic in the field, examined how schools educate working-class boys to graduate to working-class jobs. It demonstrates how 'the lads' are pigeon-holed and attack a power system that is stacked against them. Among the techniques of 'resistance' against school authority that Willis identifies are indiscipline, sarcasm, larking around, being cheeky to teachers, having a 'laff', truancy and rejecting the sanctioned reward system for study. The lads refuse to 'play the game'. They ridicule the '*ear' oles*' who work co-operatively with teachers. Resistance here 'writes over' school rules, the curriculum and the promise of upward mobility through study to promote types of identity and solidarity which equate prestige with challenging the official order. The forms of resistance that Willis describes have a heroic dimension. Class troublemakers are redefined as cultural bandits and rebels. However, their acts of resistance are ultimately futile because 'the lads' unwittingly participate in a system of cultural reproduction that devalues them and ultimately places them in low status, low paid working-class jobs.

This is a brilliant study of on-location behaviour. For it shows how cultural practice is systematically positioned by unequal relations of power and representation within schools. The conscious acts of rebellion by 'the lads' unintentionally nudge them into being culturally stigmatized by the system. Trying to resist a system that devalues their *habitus* and scorns the vitality of their sense of resistance and opposition 'prepares' them for being denied opportunities for upward mobility by the very schooling system that is theoretically organized to 'improve' their life chances. The prevailing school culture positions rebels and cultural bandits to participate in engineering their own failure. Willis's account of the cultural mechanics of this process in relation to class, schooling and work surely captures enduring issues. Despite being nearly thirty years old, the study continues to point to much larger questions of class inequality, representational power and the positioning of individuals and groups in relation to scarce cultural, economic, political and social resources.

Yet, despite its many virtues, Willis's study is in many ways typical of the moment of the National-Popular. It assigns decisive importance to class and neglects issues of race and gender. It has little to say about multiple modernities or polysemy. On the contrary, it shows the lads only too well aware of their place in a system of power that is defined as conclusively weighted against them. A contemporary analysis of location must carefully recognize the insertion of cultural actors in *intertextured* cultural space. In other words it involves a body and a place in which multiple meanings are exchanged and multiple identities are recognized. But what is meant by embodiment and emplacement?

Embodiment

The concept of embodiment refers to the obvious fact that we all possess bodies. It also conveys the less obvious fact that the body is not only a physical fact, but also a cultural, social, economic and political resource and construction. Male bodies, female bodies, white bodies, non-white bodies, pierced bodies, sexy bodies, plain bodies, thin bodies, fat bodies, able-bodied people and disabled people pertain not merely to physical conditions but to a repertoire of representations and codes that place the body in culture.

Within Cultural Studies, two main approaches to the body have emerged. I call them *performative* and *attributive*. The chief difference between them turns on the amount of voluntarism each assigns to individuals and groups. Before considering them it should be noted that the concept of *voluntarism* refers to the freedom that individuals possess to realize personal choice.

Performative approaches to embodiment stress the *positioning* of the body in relation to discourse, representation and authority. They are associated with the writings of Jacques Lacan (1970), Michel Foucault (1970, 1977) and Judith Butler (1993, 1999). Although there are many significant differences between these writers, all hold that voluntarism is heavily conditioned by power. Butler (1993: 7) writes about individuals as installed in a 'matrix' of power relations that 'precede' the emergence of 'the human'. This sounds somewhat abstract and, to be sure, the philosophical ramifications that follow from it operate at a very high altitude and are very demanding. However, at the heart of it is the proposition that, at an unconscious level, individuals 'perform' to the requirements of systems of cultural authority that precede their existence as individual human beings. For example, girls are not simply biologically different to boys. They are culturally different too. The cultural differences between the sexes are not 'natural'. On the contrary, they derive from the systems of cultural authority and representation in which individual babies are positioned as 'boy' or 'girl'.

The performative approach to embodiment raises many questions. If action is really a matter of 'performing' to the logic of systems of cultural authority, in what sense can individuals be said to 'act'? For if individuals are positioned to perform according to the dictates of power, in what sense might they be said to be 'free'?

Attributive approaches to the body recognize that individuals and groups are positioned in relation to systems of authority, but acknowledge greater levels of voluntarism in human action. They are associated with the writings of Erving Goffman (1959), Pierre Bourdieu (1984) and Dick Hebdige (1979). Again it must be noted that there are many significant variations between these authors. However, basic to their work is the proposition that embodiment involves the conscious search for what Bourdieu (1984) calls *distinction*.

We can illustrate this briefly by using the term *embodied habitus*, developed from Bourdieu's cultural sociology, to encapsulate the relation between bodily values and symbols and social structures. As we have noted, Bourdieu's term *habitus* refers to the generative principles – rules, ways of seeing the world, schemes of classification and values – that we acquire as a normal part of living in our communities. *Habitus* is directly influenced by scarcity, since different communities are placed in contrasting relations with respect to economic, cultural, political and social resources. *Habitus* conditions behaviour. But it is not exactly right to think of it as external to the individual. The rules, ways of seeing the world, schemes of classification and values that we acquire through membership of community may precede us, but the only way of exchanging and internalizing them is through bodily interaction.

The term *embodied habitus* is designed to highlight the fact that *habitus* is engrained in the body. We do not merely inhabit communities, we 'speak' communities through the language of the body. If you are born into a Muslim fundamentalist family, the 'design' and appearance of your body will conform to the rituals of coding and representation venerated by Islam; just as if you are born into a typical consumerist Western family your dress, ways of framing the world, values and preoccupations will reflect the *habitus* in which you are positioned. You may come to dismiss this coding and system of representation in later life. But before you are able to exert an independent conscience, you go through a process of *acculturation* that involves, to begin with at least, conforming to the aesthetic protocol and ideal of the family and community to which you belong. Acculturation means internalizing the values, outlooks and behavioural practices of the culture to which you are attached through birth and growing up.

Bourdieu was also interested in how the body is organized actively and consciously as a representation to communicate *distinction*. Much of everyday life revolves around performance designed to achieve distinction. The choice of style and fashion in everyday cultural exchange is a way of making the body perform so as to achieve selected values of *recognition* and *exclusion*. By *recognition* is meant voluntary compliance with shared codes of belonging and narratives of solidarity. *Exclusion* refers to how these codes and narratives are classified by others as signifying difference or, in some cases, opposition.

The attributive approach assigns higher levels of voluntarism to human action. But it is ambivalent about how much freedom individuals really possess. Perhaps this ambivalence is calculated, for if one allows that coding, representation and theming are central to cultural processes it follows that they are crucial in the organization of identity. If this is correct, freedom is a densely conditioned concept that ultimately needs to be addressed in relation to the position of individuals with respect to economic, cultural, political and social scarcity. Notwithstanding that, attributive approaches recognize that *habitus* patterns behaviour. But, compared with the performative tradition, they recognize a greater capacity for individuals to make a difference. For example, in Hebdige's work (1979), style is the expression of subculture, but it is taken for granted that individuals have the capacity to modify cultural performance in innovative ways.

Consider the case of tattooing and piercing. Generalizing somewhat, both cultural practices signify danger and transgression. This is because each is traditionally associated with poverty. Traditionally, the lowest income groups have resorted to these methods to communicate a level of transparent distinction that the economically disadvantaged would otherwise be unable to achieve. In non-Western cultures, tattooing and piercing are applied to signify types of social inclusion and exclusion usually relating to tribal systems of belonging. Western subcultures have appropriated this repertoire of coding and redefined it to apply to urban-industrial conditions. In contemporary culture, tattooing and piercing are subject to *bricolage*. They are used and refined by relatively economically advanced groups and subcultures, and re-assigned to convey urban-industrial types of difference and distinction. Performativity here suggests greater levels of cultural awareness, since embodiment is being applied in a complex urban-industrial mosaic of styles and positions, to express individual and group distinction.

For example, Goth culture, which emerged in the post-punk scene in the late 1970s and has developed into an established urban-industrial subculture, employs body piercing, tattoos, bondage items, white make-up and black clothing to express non-violent, passive and tolerant values. Fashion accessories include black lipstick, black nail varnish, finger joint rings, long coats, pentagrams, capes, frills, silk, velvet, lace-up trousers, latex leather and metal spikes (see figure 6.2). The psychology behind this is that the items that alarm most people, or seem pointless to them in the sense of being made obsolete by cultural and technological change, expose the capitulation of the masses to the programmed diet of consumer culture. Aesthetically, Goth culture is dense with references to depression, death and rebirth. White facial make-up, black eye-shadow and black clothing are designed to express the general notion of selecting what might be called a *posthumous existence*.[1] That is, the representational codes of Goth culture might be said to symbolize some form of life after death. But what is held to be dead or dying, and what are the Goths seeking to nurture?

Fig. 6.2   Goth girl © Jamie Evans

Although the aesthetic codes of Goth culture are dismissed by several critics as proof of mindless conformity, Goths see themselves as supreme individualists. They would reject the proposition that their embodied style is an expression of performative culture. Instead they would emphasize that it expresses a set of conscious oppositional values that challenge mainstream Western culture. In particular, they reject the militarism of the Western nation-state, which climaxes today in the occupation of Iraq, and seek to open and inhabit a cultural space that is situated beyond the membrane of consumer culture. White make-up and black eye-shadow are doubly coded. Among other things, they signify both the impending death of consumer culture and the militarism that ultimately underpins it. Consumption implies paid employment. The extreme facial insignia of the Goths is likely to weaken their position in the labour market rather than enhance it, since most mainstream Western employers are likely to regard it as aberrant or transgressive. Similarly, facial piercing and white make-up are anti-militaristic, since facial chains and rings offer additional gripping points for combatants, and white make-up makes individuals more conspicuous and, thus, a clearer target for the enemy. The facial insignia of the Goths signifies refusal to participate in consumer culture and alienation from the values of militarism. The Goth aesthetic of embodiment works by defining itself in opposition to the prestigious, stock values revered by orthodox consumers as healthy and attractive, such as buying the latest market commodity and being consciously influenced by advertising and marketing. For Goths, it is the refusal of consumers to readily acknowledge that pain, death and suffering are a legitimate part of life that exposes their ultimate lack of realism. Hence, Goths regard consumers to be victims of a form of consumerist brainwashing from which the Goths are liberated by their dress and state of mind.

The desire for distinction and individualism runs deep in contemporary culture. To many, the appearance of the Goths may seem to constitute an extreme case in this respect, one that, indeed, borders on the morbid and pathological. Their individualism is too extreme and their codes of representation of difference are too inflexible. However, precisely because of this, an exploration of their aesthetics and state of mind has broader implications in clarifying general cultural trends. For on closer inspection, cultural extremity is invariably connected with less accentuated or pronounced social and cultural types of resistance. Discrete piercing and tattooing can probably be found in every schoolroom, lecture hall and workplace. They may be read as representing individuality and difference in a culture dominated by consumer conformity and passive acceptance of militarism. Embodiment here is constituted, very deliberately, as a sign of resistance, even if it is outwardly coded as merely 'fashion'. Tattooing and piercing makes the body 'speak'. Even if what it 'says' is not immediately understood, the statement of running upstream from real or idealized forms of conformity is an element in the interplay of culture.

Of course, the question remains how far these options for the body are patterned by performative culture (in Butler's sense of the term), and how far they reflect personal choice. It may be that this question can never be resolved. For Butler's idea of performativity ultimately rests upon the proposition that individuals and groups are compelled by dynamics that are located at a profoundly *unconscious* level. The unconscious may be said to influence conscious life but, by definition, it operates below the horizon of awareness and can therefore never be fully accessed. But some light can be shed on the subject if we turn again to the topic of the violation of codes and expectations, which we raised in discussing the Michael Jackson case.

Remember, the principle here is that the hand of power in governing our values and outlooks is revealed most sharply when these values and outlooks are inverted or violated. Perhaps we can gain an insight into the relationship between embodiment and performativity by examining cases where bodily experience is violated. For when a body starts to obey different rules through illness or accident, the 'normal' rules governing cultures of embodiment are likely to be thrown into sharper relief since the 'new' condition of the body is incompatible with them.

A personal example may serve here. My former partner for over two decades, Gerry, was diagnosed with Parkinson's disease in 1995. Parkinson's disease is a progressive neurological illness produced when the brain ceases to generate dopamine. Among the symptoms are rigidity in the body, problems in swallowing and blinking, decreasing mobility, dyskinesia (body tremors), sleeplessness, anxiety, hypertension and the impediment of respiratory functions. The symptoms are not the same for everybody, just as the rate of physical decline varies between individuals. Doctors use a variety of drugs to control the progress of the disease. Each comes with a distinctive, and sometimes alarming, set of side effects. For example, a drug designed to enhance mobility may increase dyskinesia, intensifying bobbing motions of the head and shaking of the arms and neck. Gerry's symptoms included acute panic attacks that were so severe that she mistook them for heart attacks, partial paralysis, 'freezing' or the inability to move, breathing difficulties, an inability to sleep on a soft surface like a mattress because it admitted no leverage to turn over or change position, a violent reaction to loud noises, difficulty in handwriting, rapid and severe changes in body temperature, the freezing of facial muscles, sleeplessness and temporary obsessional states based, for example, in the conviction that her legs were floating away from her body. The consequences of these symptoms are real enough. But they turn the body into a kind of 'fictive' state in which things that were formerly impossible (your legs floating away from the body) become entertained as real possibilities and 'you' become a spectator of the tricks and turns of the mad impresario who controls your bodily functions.

With the passage of time, experience of these symptoms and the development of self-medication strategies to the prescribed drug regime, a degree of control over the illness was achieved. But management of Parkinson's disease is complicated by the unpredictability of the symptoms. A person can 'go off' in minutes and 'come on' just as rapidly. In the state of 'coming on' a condition of quasi-normality is restored. This induces states of temporary near well-being among people. But they are never permanent. Moreover, the struggle to combat symptoms is waged in the disheartening knowledge that the disease is irreversible and, indeed, is bound to get worse in time. This, together with the effects of some of the drugs, induces a more or less permanent state of anxiety and dread.

Some of the symptoms leave the sufferer vulnerable in highly practical ways. For example, Gerry 'froze' in a busy shopping mall and felt that she was a conspicuous target for muggers. Freezing can also produce bizarre experiences that have a humorous side. Once Gerry 'froze' on an underground train and could not leave her seat, which made her miss a meeting. On other occasions, it was less easy to be light hearted. Once, when walking slowly down a street, Gerry was physically shoved aside by a young man because she was in his way. What do you do in this situation? Complain that you are suffering from a debilitating disease that impedes movement? Reproach the man for his lack of manners? Or just shrug and get on with it? A sense of humour is an asset in these trying circumstances.

Eventually, Gerry resigned from a responsible job as Chief Executive for Guide Dogs For The Blind and worked part time in another senior area of the voluntary sector. Her new life involved the development of unaccustomed rituals like 'booting up' in the mornings – a period of between 40 and 80 minutes while the drugs restored mobility – prolonged periods of sleeplessness and, of course, the treadmill of taking a variety of drugs every two hours.

You might argue over how much of Gerry's struggles with the condition of Parkinson's are a matter of a sort of localized performativity (the advice and expectations given by doctors) and how much she uses her voluntary insights to respond to the illness as a 'new (unwelcome) world'. What cannot be argued about, at least from my position, is that however large the concern and assistance of carers, it is the individual alone who has to struggle with the anxieties and frustrations of the various distressing and unpredictable symptoms of the disease. It is the individual alone who labels the symptoms in terms of her own code, which frequently involves rejecting or modifying the advice of doctors and nurses. For example, Gerry altered the consultant's prescribed drug regimes by taking less of one drug and more of another, and by altering the sequencing of taking the drugs. Instead of performing like a 'cultural dope'[2] she acted as a person trying to make sense of her own body. The sense I get as a witness of another's chronic illness is one of personal ingenuity, not the droneship of conforming to medical advice, and inventiveness in redefining your altered body in a world that is typically uncomprehending. To this extent, the greater voluntarism to personal behaviour recognized by the attributive approach to the body is validated. For despite the active, material force that disability constitutes, the patient ultimately understands and seeks to manage it in their own fashion.

It is trite to observe that there are innate physical difficulties in coping with Parkinson's disease. There are many cultural and social problems that arise because the body is coded by others in a different way. The person with the illness also learns to be doubly divided from the able-bodied person they were and from able-bodied others who are apt now to be represented and experienced as citizens from another state. What we are dealing with here is a profound clash of cultures. The person with the disease starts from a different place, faces a different horizon of challenges and literally begins to move and think in a different way than the rest of us. Culturally speaking, the most important thing about Parkinson's disease is that the sufferer and her carers know what the symptoms mean while others have only a hazy idea or are oblivious. Thus, swaying, shuffling and stumbling, which others may 'see' as indications of drunkenness, are in reality effects of dyskinesia. Slurred speech, which may generally suggest mental impairment or a stroke, is in reality often a temporary effect of a given drug regime; lack of breath, giddiness and immobility, which may generally indicate thrombosis, is in reality a panic attack. To put it at its simplest, illness is transforming the culture of the body in ways that conflict with general and therefore 'typical' codes of normal embodiment. The problem is not so much that most people don't know about the symptoms of the disease, it is that the general codes governing embodiment in everyday life require us to pay attention only to a limited repertoire of information.

Embodiment, then, carries all sorts of clues about culture. The examination of physical form, dress and hairstyle reveals much about how persons and groups are situated in relation to scarce resources. Make-up, piercing, tattooing, clothes and cosmetics refer directly to how the body is represented and, as such, reveal a good deal about distinction. Physical illness may expose the narrow limitations of conventional codes of embodiment. They may indeed reveal the performative character of culture but only by a struggle with these codes that is intensely personal. In all cases, the positioning of the body in culture is of decisive importance in cultural analysis. The mechanics of this positioning, and its relation to the power relations between groups and individuals, brings us to the related question of emplacement in culture.

Emplacement

Emplacement simply means the position that individuals and groups occupy in relation to *resources*. By the term 'resources' is meant economic, cultural, social and political capital. Capital here is understood as a type of value. As such, it is bound up with relations of power. Unequal power relations constitute the primary milieu in which individual action occurs. If *habitus* refers to generative principles – conceptual frameworks, schemes of classification and ways of positioning ourselves in the world – power refers to how these assets are valued in society and culture. Emplacement directly influences embodiment since it conditions the resources that are allocated to diet, clothing, education, housing, travel, transport and health care. Embodiment and emplacement situate us in *locations* that pattern the trajectories of behaviour that we pursue.

There are very obvious ways in which the cultural significance of emplacement can be studied. For example, comparative analysis of national conditions reveals huge differences in mortality, education and health care between countries. In Zimbabwe the current average life expectancy of males and females is 33.3 and 32.6 years respectively. This has *declined* from 57.4 and 62.6 years in 1990, and 39.7 and 42 years in 2000 (www.un.commondatabase.globalis.guv.unuedu). Why? A combination of political and economic factors are involved. Chief among them are the policies developed by Robert Mugabe's Zanu PF (Zimbabwe African National Union Patriotic Front) government which have created a deterioration in living conditions. In particular, the compulsory land reform measures that transferred land ownership from whites to the peasantry, bureaucratic corruption, political repression by the government and inadequate policies to manage the HIV/AIDS epidemic have resulted in a negative impact.

Because most of us, in the West, are inured to a culture that theoretically delivers constant progress, we find cases of national cultural and economic decline shocking. But Zimbabwe is by no means alone. For example, in Liberia a mixture of state corruption, internal conflict, HIV/ AIDS problems and the decline of agriculture has resulted in an average life expectancy for males and females of 47 years. Average per capita income in 2003 was estimated to be $130 (www.unicef.org/infocountry). Throughout Africa, South East Asia, parts of the former Soviet Union and Latin America cases of extreme poverty are readily found.

Emplacement, then, conditions access to scarce resources and fundamentally influences personal life expectancy. In Western culture, class, gender, ethnicity, nation, status and subculture are the primary influences positioning individuals and groups in relation to scarce resources. The basic component of emplacement is the family. The economic, cultural, social and political capital of your parents influences the trajectory of life that you will follow. Families are located within communities that, in turn, are part of classes, regions and nations. The relationships between emplacement and cultural practice can be profitably studied at each of these levels.

For example, Paul Gilroy's writings on race and power (1987, 1993) demonstrate how racial emplacement directly influences access to scarce resources. His early work explores how the law in Britain developed the stereotype of black criminality (Gilroy 1987). Gilroy argues that in the early 1950s policing the black population was relatively relaxed. The law operated with *some* stereotypes, notably that the black population is more likely to be involved in gambling and prostitution. But the suggestion of a black population polarized against the interests of the white mainstream scarcely figured in the media or public life.

It was not until the 1960s, as part of a backlash to overcrowding and housing shortages, that the black population began to be stigmatized as 'alien' and 'threatening' to the national way of life. Many sections of the British media fuelled and pandered to popular prejudice by representing black youth as work-shy, violent and dishonest. In particular, mugging started be portrayed as a predominantly black crime. This culminated in demands for increased policing in black neighbourhoods and tougher sentencing. As we shall see later in the chapter, the drift towards 'a law and order society' in the 1970s and 1980s reflected a reaction to the permissive society of the 1960s and, at a deeper level, was connected to frictions in the character of the British nation-state (Hall et al. 1978; Hall 1979). Gilroy's work suggested that the judiciary, police and media operated with the construct of the 'racialized Other' with respect to the black population. Increased levels of surveillance, the quasi-covert expectation in the media and police control rooms of 'trouble' in black neighbourhoods and harsher sentencing combined to inflame race relations.

In later work, Gilroy (1993) modified his approach to racial emplacement from a polarized model between whites and blacks to a more 'hybrid', 'creolized' view. He uses 'the Black Atlantic' as a metaphor for a complex unity of racial mixture in which many forms of mixing, blending and antagonism are apparent. The emplacement of successive waves of black immigrants on both sides of the Atlantic through immigration is regarded as creating hybrid identities; that is, identities that recognize racial mixture. The implication is that conventional models of racial emplacement in North American and Western European societies are too crude. Racial identities are not fixed. They are in perpetual movement. Gilroy argues that hybrid identity may be examined at the cultural level by exploring popular artistic form, such as rap, hip hop or the novels of Ellison, Morrison, Walker and Baldwin. In this sense music and literature act as direct representations of issues of emplacement and, of course, embodiment. This work reflects the influence of the Textual-Representational and Global/Post-Essentialist moments in Cultural Studies and the turn away from the national-popular focus.

But globalization also raises a separate set of questions for emplacement, having to do with the *dematerialization* of culture. By the term 'dematerialization' is meant the replacement of solid relations by transparent ones. Marx and Engels (1848: 38) nicely captured this in the poetic phrase 'all that is solid melts into air', which has now perhaps become a cliché of Cultural Studies and Sociology. The phrase may sound like double Dutch. But it refers to a prominent characteristic of globalization, and it changes how we should think about cultural emplacement. What is being driven at here is the tendency of some aspects of global culture to take on an ever greater virtual form: the replacement of phone calls with texts; the switch from High Street banking to internet banking; the replacement of the CD with computer downloads of recorded music; and the growth of e-culture as a major channel of communication. Some of the challenges that this presents for how emplacement should be understood in Cultural Studies can be clarified by focusing on the example of intellectual property.

Intellectual property has been defined by the World Intellectual Property Organization (WIPO) as 'the products of the mind: inventions, literary and artistic works, any symbols, names, images and designs used in commerce' (quoted by Davis 2003: 2). It is a pivotal category in popular culture since the exchange of recorded music, film, literature, fashion and many other cultural forms involving financial transactions between a producer and consumer turn upon the assertion of copyright. This sounds straightforward: You go into a music store. You buy a CD. The retailer gains an income from the sale and so do the record company and recording artist(s). But globalization is standing this relationship on its head. It is multiplying opportunities for primary and secondary copyright infringement.

Primary copyright infringement occurs when a person initiates, or authorizes another to initiate, any of the restricted acts protected by the assertion of copyright. Secondary infringement refers to selling, exhibiting, distributing or manufacturing infringed works. How is globalization producing new opportunities for these illegal acts? Essentially the computer and the web emplace the consumer differently in the marketplace and alter the conventional relationship between producers and consumers. They allow for the illegal transformation and exchange of copyrighted works with negligible risk of detection.

In recent years, the question of exchange has been dramatically illustrated by the continuing dispute over Peer-To-Peer (P2P) net file exchange that enables consumers to illegally download copyrighted materials. File exchange companies like Napster, eDonkey, Kazaa, Morpheus and XoloX offer efficient, low cost file exchange services. Illegal downloading is depressing the sales of multinational record companies. The International Federation of the Phonographic Industry (IFPI) Piracy Report (June 2005) reported that one in three discs sold worldwide is an illegal copy (www.ifpi.org). This amounts to a $4.6 billion business. CD sales have dropped by 25 per cent since file sharing began to be popularized in 1999 (*The Guardian* 6.09.05). File sharing raises a number of difficult questions about access, intellectual property and fair use.

The response of the recording industry has been to reassert the inviolable character of copyright. The IFPI Piracy Report noted that 14,227 legal actions against illegal file sharing had been taken by the summer of 2005. The Recording Industry Association of America (RIAA) has pursued a parallel track in the USA. The industry marshals a policy of zero tolerance. However, practically speaking, legal action is no more than the tip of the iceberg. It is estimated that there are over 40 million P2P network users in the USA alone (Davis 2003: 157). Currently, there is no effective system of global policing in place. Litigation is therefore a random strategy that leaves most illegal downloaders unaffected and, in addition, runs the risk of unintentionally producing consumer martyrs. Levine (2004: 16–17) cites the case of Brianna LaHara, a 12-year-old American Catholic schoolgirl, who was threatened with a multi-million dollar law suit for downloading sitcom soundtracks and nursery jingles,

like *If You're Happy And You Know It*. The case was eventually settled
for $2000, but not without much negative publicity for the RIAA and
their clients. Conversely, the RIAA might respond that litigation succeeded in nailing the charge of illegality to the file-sharing pioneer
Napster and forced it to introduce a fee-paying system. Launched in
1999, Napster was the most potent symbol of neat net banditry. In effect,
it was a global supermarket in which consumers were free to exchange
and download filed music at no cost. Goldstein (2003: 166) estimates
that at its peak Napster provided services for 70 million illegal downloaders. Eventually, legal action forced Napster to cease trading and
re-launch itself as a legal fee-paying downloading service. The RIAA has
also supported legal action designed to prevent the manufacturers of
technology that enables the circumvention of copyright making their
products available to the public. The US Digital Millennium Copyright
Act (DMCA), passed in 1998, is a controversial piece of blanket legisla-
tion that criminalizes the production and distribution of technology with
the capacity to circumvent copyright and increases penalties for copyright infringement. Designated 'legitimate' parties, such as libraries,
archives and educational institutions, are allowed limited exemption. By
and large, the Act has been supported by the entertainment and software
industries and opposed by librarians, academics and consumer groups
on the grounds that it inhibits freedom of information.

Penalizing companies that produce circumvention technologies has
achieved some success. In June 2005 the US Supreme Court ruled against
Grokster and StreamCast Networks, both makers of P2P software, in
finding that they are liable for what users do with their software. In
effect, the ruling found the companies guilty of inducing consumers to
engage in copyright infringement. Similarly, in September 2005 the Australian Federal Court ordered Kazaa, the world's biggest file-sharing
service, to filter copyrighted material from its network. Multinationals
in the film and recording industry applauded the decisions as signalling
a decisive change in the judiciary's position on the illegality of P2P file-
sharing systems. But it is not that simple or straightforward.

In the first place, the rulings misunderstand that P2P file sharing is
now an *established* method of consuming music and film. The Cambridge company Cachel Logic estimates that P2P file sharing is currently
the main source of data traffic on the net. Depending on the time of day,
volumes range between two and ten times those of other web traffic
(Naughton 2005). In view of this level of activity, it is hard to see how
the judiciary and police can mount a credible policy of monitoring and
prosecuting every illegal downloader. Instead, what the closure of

file-sharing services like Grokster, StreamCast and Kazaa is likely to accomplish is simply the migration of file-sharers to more capable P2P programmes.

Another big issue is that software companies will inevitably challenge the ruling against technologies that permit inducement of copyright infringement on the grounds that it imperils innovation. What technology company worth its salt will pour millions of pounds into Research and Development programmes to improve software, if they might be sued by a copyright holder over which they have no control?

The rulings also raise doubt about the legality of the principle of 'fair use'. With certain provisos, European and North American law has allowed for 'fair use' of copyright material in the following cases (Davis 2003; Goldstein 2003):

1 Research or private study, provided that no more than one copy is reproduced.
2 Criticism or review provided that appropriate recognition of the original source is made.
3 Reporting of current events, provided that appropriate acknowledgement of the original source is made. Acknowledgement is not necessary in cases of reporting done via a live sound recording, broadcast or cable programme.

Curtailing these uses would have profound consequences for the conduct of democracy and the quality of public life. If the media or general public could not refer critically to literature, film or music on the grounds that to do so infringes copyright, the effect would be to drastically reduce free speech, the exchange of ideas and the conduct of the free press. A raft of separate questions concerning civil liberties and the public responsibilities of multinationals would be launched in taking this action.

This in turn raises the matter of whether record and cinema multinationals are justified in asserting copyright over use *after* the point of sale. The multinationals condemn P2P exchange as a pernicious cultural technology because it erodes profit margins. But there is another way of looking at it. P2P exchange may be viewed as a *gift relationship*. Individuals make the CD and film files that they legally own available on the net for downloading. It may be legitimate to penalize companies who make a profit from the exchange service to continue trading. But there are difficulties in extending the principle to individuals. For one thing, it interferes with the American Constitution's First Amendment that guarantees free speech and press. The relevant principle here is that copyright monopoly must not prohibit cultural exchange that benefits all. More widely, why should intellectual property be treated differently to any other commodity? If I buy a pot plant and make cuttings for my mother, the garden centre has no legal basis to claim that I am depriving the garden nursery of future sales. It is not self-evident that the copyright holders over intellectual property have a privileged claim over the owners of garden nurseries. For copying, imitation, sampling and parody of copyrighted works may enlarge and enrich culture by transforming the form of the original. Through this means, it may *increase* demand for the original by demonstrating its appeal and versatility. Indeed, many aspects of the argument have been examined by various lawsuits that allege copyright infringement over allegations of copying, sampling and parody. For example, in 1990 the music publisher Acuff-Rose Music filed a suit against the controversial rap group 2 Live Crew for copyright infringement over the Roy Orbison–William Dees song, *Oh Pretty Woman*. The group recorded their own version of the song and included it on their latest album without securing copyright clearance. Lawyers for 2 Live Crew argued that the group's version of the song did not infringe copyright because it constituted a *parody* of the original. Although their version starts with the same lyrics it quickly substitutes them with new lyrics and a play on words. For example, where the original refers to a pretty woman walking down the street, the 2 Live Crew version refers to a 'big hairy woman', 'a bald-headed woman' and a 'two-timin' woman'. In the event, the Court found in favour of the defence on the grounds that 2 Live Crew is an anti-establishment rap group who have the legal right to exercise parody in deflating cultural icons (Goldstein 2003: 2–3).

Computers and the net emplace private individuals in a new relationship of empowerment to globally access and distribute information. Equally, they introduce unprecedented levels of vulnerability for rightsholders who wish to protect their works from unauthorized use. We are at a juncture where an arrangement must be struck between these contradictory interests. The development of the cultural technology of downloading has made illegality the potential consequence of merely maximizing the functionality of the computer and the net. Multinationals recognize that this technology cannot be dis-invented. They have forged licensing arrangements with new legal digital download outputs like the Apple I-Tunes Music Store, Sony Music Store and Virgin Music Store, which have exploited the fresh opportunities of net downloading. Yet this hardly solves the problem of illegality. Legal digital downloads will always be in the minority as long as there is no effective system of policing the net.

The example shows that emplacement has a global dimension. It is perfectly legitimate for students of Cultural Studies to investigate how emplacement operates with relation to conditions of class, ethnicity, gender, subculture and nation. Focusing on a national or local level will doubtless provide many important insights into how emplacement makes you a bishop, a knight or a pawn in cultural interchange. However, now, more than ever before, the national and the local interpenetrate with the global. The case of P2P exchange and intellectual property shows how someone living in their own apartment in Lagos or Mumbai can directly influence the profit margin of a record or film company based in Hollywood or London. It provides a lesson for Cultural Studies to examine the role of new technologies in creating global cultural clusters that are invisible but have the power to affect economics, politics and culture.

Context

The embodiment and emplacement of an individual in a particular location presupposes not merely an immediate relationship but a historical and structural one. The resources in the locations that we occupy are situated in a *context*. The term 'context' in this respect has two meanings. Firstly, it refers to the general power structure that allocates resources through institutions designed to achieve *normative coercion*. The term 'normative coercion' simply means the normal types of behaviour in everyday life that we are encouraged and persuaded to apply irrespective of the economic, political and cultural milieu in which we are located and the *habitus* from which we originate. Normative coercion covers everything from table manners and highway etiquette to the character of our beliefs in justice and freedom. Analytically, Cultural Studies has been particularly interested in the roles of institutions like the police, judiciary, schools, the media and the state in the practice of normative coercion. Through these gateways individuals are positioned in relation to dominant structures of power. They do so, not by capitulating to power in the crude sense of recognizing subordination, but by the infinitely more subtle and flexible means of learning to adopt the myth of themselves as 'free agents'.

The second meaning of the term 'context' refers to the historical and structural dimensions behind location, emplacement and embodiment. The cultural associations and signs that are attached to specific types of embodiment and emplacement, and the unequal allocation of resources to different locations, have a past and a structure. This is examined with respect to economics, society, politics and culture at both the national and global levels. On-location behaviour, embodiment and emplacement are coloured by political economy. What does it mean to be *coloured* by political economy?

Through being in culture, and making culture with others, individuals change cultural relations. Within class or gender divisions, individuals are positioned in relation to scarce resources in diverse and mixed ways. This is sometimes missed in accounts that approach culture as the reflection of primary influences in the formation of context such as class, gender, nation and race. The concept of context used here assumes a constant interplay between these forces. By paying attention to the *situated dynamics* between location, embodiment, emplacement and context in cultural analysis, we stand the chance of adding to our understanding of the internal divisions in class, gender and race as well as highlighting the significance of tradition and space in cultural practice. At the 'Crossroads' International conference held at the University of Illinois at Urbana-Champaign in 2004, a major theme was the need for Cultural Studies to relate culture to political economy. The study of cultural phenomena can be so absorbing that we become mesmerised by content, and disassociate cultural practice from context. Cultural Studies then risks deteriorating into a sort of blogging pool in which people focus narrowly on their own enthusiasms and the cultural genres associated with them.

Are there any models that we can follow to ensure that cultural investigation achieves constant interplay between practice, content and context? Hall et al.'s *Policing the Crisis* (1978) is often referred to as a classic of the National-Popular moment in Cultural Studies. But the significance of the attempt it makes to link practice, content and context extends well beyond this period in the history of the discipline. As a model it offers many lessons that have still not been fully explored.

What makes the study a benchmark in the field? Above all it is the attention to the issue that the personal in cultural form and content is in perpetual interplay with the state and the market. To put it differently, cultural practice is always inscribed with political and economic power. The central features of cultural life, such as where on-location behaviour occurs, how embodiment is encoded, why some cultural genres emerge and others fall by the wayside and the relationship between emplacement and scarcity are enmeshed with the situated dynamics of the context patterned by the market and the state.

Appropriately, the birth of this study lay in the media. Researchers in the Birmingham Centre for Contemporary Cultural Studies alighted upon an isolated newspaper report on the sentencing of three youths for the apparently random mugging of a male in Birmingham. Local figures in the community bemoaned the sentence of twenty years for the 'ring-leader' and ten years each for his associates as excessive. The satisfaction that most of the media exhibited at the sentencing, and the alarmist language referring to the rising urban threat posed by ethnic, jobless youth was duly noted. This concrete item from contemporary culture stimulated, firstly, detailed research into how the incident was represented in the press and, secondly, intensive research into the historical statistics on mugging in Britain. Media representations were related to anxieties about the Americanization of British life, in particular the connection between the apparent rise of violent gang formations in youth subcultures. The upshot of the historical analysis was that the newspaper report was judged to be factually incorrect in suggesting a rising tide of violence. According to the statistics, the incidence of mugging was *in decline* when the assault took place. Borrowing Stanley Cohen's concepts of 'moral panic' and 'media amplification' (1972), Hall and his associates argued that the media *exaggerated* the gathering hazard posed by youth culture to public safety. The question then became why this exaggeration was taking place.

In an ambitious and hugely impressive sweep of historical and cultural analysis, the answer was traced back to the crisis in the British state. Criss-crossing decades, and supporting the analysis with a wealth of compelling historical data, *Policing the Crisis* framed the debate on law and order around the rise of 'the representative-interventionist state' between the 1880s and 1920s. From this time, the British state was portrayed as engaged in a constant 'war of manoeuvre' to win the consent of the working class. This involved a 'complex unity' of political coalitions and concessions to civil society. It was a response to a series of pressures 'from below', and from global competition, which eroded the power of the traditional laissez-faire state. The long tail of concessions culminated in the postwar settlement in which all the major political parties recognized a commitment to the managed economy and the welfare state.

This commitment is understood in terms of the concept of *hegemony*. As we saw earlier, hegemony operates through positioning and persuasion. It makes concessions to rising groups and classes, but in doing so positions them in relations of dependency and, perhaps one might say, *latent* challenge to the governing power bloc. The postwar welfare settlement recognized the right of the working class to health care, education and full employment. But it stopped well short of assigning unlimited power to the people. Instead the working class was positioned in a *new* relation to scarcity with the state acting as a gate-keeper to extract greater resources from the market for public distribution. Positioning under hegemony assumes that individuals, groups and classes will remain located in their place as a consequence of being assigned new resources. It is this commitment, based on high levels of taxation and state regulation, that created free health and education services at the point of delivery and contributed to the relaxation of social and cultural attitudes that was tested in the 1960s with the rise of the so-called 'permissive society'. Among its primary features were the liberalization of laws prohibiting homosexuality; wider social acceptance of cohabitation over marriage; the de-stigmatization of divorce; the recognition of multi-ethnic difference; and the acceptance that Britain's colonial heritage involved exploitation and repression. For Hall and his associates it was the conviction that the permissive society had gone too far that was at the root of the moral panic against mugging in the 1970s. Media representations about the Americanization of British life reflected anxieties about the depletion and loss of national identity.

Later, in the 1980s, the Thatcher–Reagan new Right deplored 'the nanny state' for creating a comfort-zone culture in which ambition and enterprise were held to be dissipated by punitive levels of taxation to fund state 'hand-outs' in education, welfare and the arts. They called for the revival of independence, self-reliance, rolling back state expenditure, lower taxes and the restoration of nationalist values. Although subsequent governments in the anglophone world have been critical of many aspects of the Reagan–Thatcher years, they have not sought to reverse the central values of support for self-reliance, controlling state expenditure and restoring national pride. To be sure, many leading players have continued the international policing role pursued by Thatcher and Reagan.

As Hall and his associates predicted in *Policing the Crisis*, the hidden agenda behind this was the substitution of the permissive society with the 'law and order society'. Central to the latter was an enlarged police force with greater powers of policing, toughening-up policies on welfare state 'scroungers' and illegal refugees, dismantling trade-union powers, deregulating the market and privatizing nationalized assets.

Thus, from the analysis of an isolated and apparently random act of mugging in the West Midlands, Hall and his associates unravelled a complex politics of stereotyping, scapegoating, representation and co-option involving the crisis in British state power dating back to the turn of the nineteenth century. In doing so they pitchforked public debate on mugging from a simple moral issue to the economic, political and ideological conditions producing crime. The core Birmingham questions of how power underwrites privilege and ideology organizes identities and values were pursued in a tightly organized, sustained analysis which was both compelling and forceful. Many other important studies on schooling, race, sexual inequality and the media emerged from the Birmingham Centre. But none matched *Policing the Crisis* in combining historical rigour and contemporary politics with penetrating cultural analysis. In particular, the book demonstrated that a critical reading of apparently meaningless contemporary cultural events can lead to the unmasking of power and, through this, the elucidation of how identity and action is 'summoned' or called into being.

At the level of national politics and economics, the 'summoning' of identity and action was interpreted by drawing upon Althusser's concept of *interpellation* (1971). Althusser's sources for this concept were complex. Central to them was the question of how individuals are constructed as social subjects. How do we learn to regard ourselves as independent individuals even when most of our actions are governed by being positioned in relation to forces of power of one kind or another? Where do our ethical beliefs and ideas of distributive justice come from? Althusser submitted that individuals are actually the 'bearers' of power structures rather than free actors. The normative institutions of coercion – schools, the judiciary, medicine, the police – act as the switchboard between the interests behind hegemony and individuals who are constructed to regard themselves as 'autonomous'. Although swings and balances are part and parcel of the process, the thrust of hegemony is to reproduce capitalist relations of power. Althusser and Hall et al. were each operating in the Marxist tradition. They assumed that hegemony operated to reproduce citizens in a position of cultural dependency with respect to dominant interests. Because the state was regarded to be at the heart of this process, it was the focal point of the cultural analysis of context. With the passing of the National-Popular moment this emphasis upon the centrality of the state has waned. The neo-liberal revival of the last quarter of a century has marginalized critics of the market and popularized the notion of *cool capitalism* (McGuigan 2006). Of course, the state still possesses huge economic and cultural power through its control of the police, the judiciary, international relations policy, licensing, taxation and the governance of public assets. But globalization has enhanced the prominence of multinational corporations in shaping the context of cultural interplay. Through branding multinationals interpellate (call forth/summon) particular models of consumer identity into which consumers are positioned and which shape on-location practice.

Modernity and postmodernity

The notion of cultural interplay has been radically extended by some critics. They argue that the rules of the game governing the relationships between cultural production, genre, consumption and cultural politics have fundamentally changed. Globalization and the acceleration of cultural change have combined to create a new type of culture. This requires the concept of context to be overhauled and adjusted. For example, Jameson (1992) famously argued that the context of contemporary culture is defined by the disintegration of the distinction between high and low culture; the replacement of artistic style with pastiche; the promiscuous mixing of genres from past and present; the subordination of politics to aesthetics; and the fashion for nostalgia. In brief, culture has moved into a new situation in which all of the fundamentals need to be rethought.

These arguments are conveniently bundled together in what has become known as the debate around modernity and postmodernity. Modernity is associated with dynamism, urban-industrial society, the money economy, competitive labour markets, the rise of the nation-state, the spread of science and rationality into every avenue of life, democracy, secularism and progress. Historians sometimes squabble about the historical seeding of modernity, but all agree that the late eighteenth-century Enlightenment was decisive in its development. A number of developments came together at this time. The Enlightenment privileged science, technology and rationality over myth, superstition, magic and religion. The American (1776) and French Revolutions (1789–99) raised equality, liberty and fraternity as values over monarchy, deference and blind obedience to tradition. The Enlightenment sought to discover universal truths about human life and apply them for the improvement of mankind. The enormous ambition of the Enlightenment to break with superstition and time-worn habit has been a long-standing subject of critical appreciation. So have the delusions of Enlightenment utopianism. Following very different paths of analysis, Adorno and Horkheimer (1944) and Foucault (1970, 1977, 1979) argued that Enlightenment rationality produced unintended forms of domination and oppression. The same logic of control that produced public parks and heart surgery created Auschwitz and the electric chair.

The crisis in modernity is typically explored and understood in cultural terms. Most famously, Lyotard (1984) refers to the collapse of the 'grand narratives' of the Enlightenment and the spoiled character of the commitment to creating universal knowledge about the human condition. In Cultural Studies this was vital in popularizing the Textual-Representational moment, since it emphasized the significance of theming, coding, intertextuality and power over notions of 'objective culture' and universal truth. If everything is coded, themed and marked by the hand of power, ideas of cultural positioning, difference and anti-essentialism are naturally strengthened. Cultural relativism emphasizes the role of language games and *habitus* in producing authority and truth. This, allied to what Lyotard (1984) memorably called 'incredulity towards grand meta-narratives', has been the defining feature of Cultural Studies in the contemporary era.

For a while in the 1980s and 1990s it was fashionable to use the term postmodernity to describe the new cultural situation. This was an umbrella term for many distinct processes. The most significant among them were an orientation to culture which recognized its fragmentary, ambivalent and conditional character; a recognition of difference; an acknowledgement of the continuous interplay between local and global processes; a perspective on culture which acknowledged hybridity and multiculturalism; the blurring of boundaries of genre and history; the prominence of the visual in cultural exchange; and, of course, profound scepticism about grand narratives, whether they be cast at the level of scientific progress or involve the unfolding of struggles of class, race and gender.

Postmodernity raised a series of new searching questions about identity. If the grand narratives of modernity have collapsed, what sense does it make any longer for people to define themselves in terms of nation, class, gender or race? The solidarities attached to these cultural distinctions are now openly queried, thus raising fresh doubts about tradition and common ground. Instead, the fashion is to analyse culture in terms of surface rather than depth, different forms of knowledge rather than universal knowledge and laws of *positioning* rather than laws of iron integrity.

Postmodernity points to a profound change in the cultural situation. It implies that Cultural Studies needs to discard its modern categories of cultural production, genre, consumption and cultural politics. At the same time, it remains unclear what kind of politics can or will emerge from this. How can difference and conditionality be used to build solidarity? If identity is no longer a useful category, how can we explain the actions of suicide bombers from the Palestine Liberation Organization fighting for a national homeland in Israel, or gays and lesbians trying to combat sexual oppression?

Questions like this led many commentators to propose that the collapse of Modernity had been seriously exaggerated. While postmodern tendencies were recognized to profoundly modify the context in which culture operates, it was now queried whether it is necessary to be either for or against the Enlightenment or to dispense with concepts of cultural depth and identity. A shift from proposing a culture of transformation to proposing a culture of ambivalence occurred. This was symbolized in Jameson's (1992) work by the use of the term 'late modernity' to describe contemporary culture; Anthony Giddens (1994) preferred the concept of 'radicalized modernity'.

Situating yourself in culture then requires several levels of work. In the first place it involves paying attention to on-location behaviour. You need to carefully observe how people behave in cultural settings and trace patterns of behaviour. These patterns may be most sharply revealed when they are disrupted. Because we live in media-saturated societies there are plenty of options to examine examples of disruption merely by following the news. I have already referred to the trial of Michael Jackson and the image adjustment that it triggered. While I was writing this section of the book, the tabloid press published photographs of the supermodel Kate Moss taking cocaine. This led to the cancellation of several of her celebrity endorsement contracts with leading fashion companies. Questions of whether she is a suitable role model for young girls or a responsible mother were aired in the media. In all of this, issues of on-location practice, emplacement, embodiment and context were constantly aired. Merely by adopting a 'newspaper form' of Cultural Studies, by taking cuttings from papers and videoing the TV news, it was possible to produce a fairly detailed account of the cultural realignment to the public image of Kate Moss.

Situating yourself in culture also means observing questions of embodiment and emplacement. Not merely how others are embodied and emplaced, but also the details of your own embodiment and emplacement. Why do you refuse to have a tattoo when it is widespread practice in your peer group? Why won't you use a mobile phone in a train carriage, or complain if someone is disturbing you by doing so? What makes you want to have an Apple iPod over all other brands? It is tempting to give naturalistic answers to all of these questions. That is, you simply happen to be the way that you are in respect of all of these issues. However, by isolating embodiment and emplacement, and relating each to issues of scarcity, the *constructed* character of your inclinations and behaviour becomes more apparent.

Although location, embodiment and emplacement are necessary features to consider in any form of Cultural Studies, they are not sufficient. They are situated in the bigger picture of *context*. That is, the social, cultural, economic and political framework in which cultural action occurs. The most valuable forms of Cultural Studies analyse and present culture as the constant interplay between these four levels. But they face additional challenges: cultural distortion and cultural change. The question of cultural change has been dealt with earlier with reference to the necessity for Cultural Studies to accept that its field of study is not static and is intrinsically open to change. It is necessary now to address the question of cultural distortion at greater length.

7

Cultural Distortion

Distortion is part of the *context* of contemporary culture. We have already noted how the media code data to encourage preferred readings of the news and other items. The purpose of these readings is to influence the context in which decisions about emplacement, embodiment and location occur. The chain of coding can be traced all the way back to the dominant power bloc in society which seeks to maintain hegemony and ensure cultural reproduction.

A case in point is the Iraq war of 2003. The Allied pretext for war was the supposed threat of biological and chemical warfare posed by Saddam Hussein's regime. Both George W. Bush and Tony Blair argued that unambiguous intelligence information existed proving that Saddam possessed a clear and present danger to the West and pro-Western countries in the Arab world. Blair told the British Parliament that Saddam possessed biological and chemical capability that could be activated 'within 45 minutes'. A complex web of innuendo and hearsay was spun in the Anglo-American media and the public to support this case. A deliberate and far-reaching attempt was made to mould the climate of public opinion in order to engineer a culture of consent. At one point, the Bush government let it be known that it suspected the Iraqis were behind anthrax attacks in the USA. When that allegation failed to be corroborated, the emphasis switched to Iraq's record of human rights violations. In particular, the extensive, verifiable Iraqi use of chemical and biological weapons in the war against Iran during the 1980s was featured prominently in state briefings. In the event, after the Allied invasion, weapons inspectors were unable to find much evidence of a significant biological and chemical weapons capacity in the country. As a result, the media widely denounced the reason for going to war as being fabricated, relying on policies of disinformation and a far-fetched view of the Iraqi threat to world peace.

Another reading of the invasion began to coalesce and acquire credence (Mann 2004; Harvey 2005). This focused on Iraq's oil reserves, which are estimated to constitute 10 per cent of the world's capacity. According to this view, the USA had a long-term strategy to secure a military presence in the Middle East in order to safeguard and regulate oil supplies. What is the evidence for this argument? After the Gulf War (1991), US presence in the region escalated. 9/11 intensified US rhetoric against the threat from Islamic fundamentalism. This underwrote the Allied campaign to overthrow the Taliban in Afghanistan in 2001.

In the aftermath, the embarrassing failure to capture Osama bin Laden created pressure for an unequivocal display of American military might in the region. In addition, the American public needed to be diverted from the economic recession that commenced early in 2001. Bush faced a domestic economy beset by rising unemployment, the plummeting value of pension funds, a serious and intractable balance of trade deficit and a welter of corporate scandals associated with accounting failures and errors of regulation that were damaging Wall Street's reputation. Oil-rich Iraq, led by an unpopular dictator, was a convenient target for American expansionist ambitions.

The hawks in Bush's cabinet denounced Iraq as an 'axis of evil' and attributed links between Saddam and Al Qaeda. These links were never corroborated. The 9/11 Commission hearings and reports and the US Senate Report on Intelligence, together with the Hutton and Butler inquiries in the UK, concluded that there were serious errors in intelligence work and systematic evasion on the part of the American and British governments.

On this reading of the Iraq war, then, the invasion was the fulfilment of long-planned American strategic interests designed to create an unassailable military presence in the central Asian republics in order to dominate Caspian Basin oil reserves. By this means, contends David Harvey (2005: 25), the USA hopes 'to keep effective control over the global economy for the next fifty years'. In Iraq the reconciliation of Kurdish, Sunni and Shi'ite divisions is still a long way off. A long-term option to deal with the challenge may be to partition Iraq into three tribal/religious states. In the interim, the Americans are proceeding pell-mell with the 'liberalization' of the Iraqi economy. In September 2003, Paul Bremner, head of the Coalition Provisional Authority, announced

a series of decrees for 'full privatization of public enterprises, full ownership rights by foreign firms of Iraqi businesses, full repatriation of foreign
profits . . . the opening of Iraq's banks to foreign control . . . the elimination of nearly all trade barriers' (quoted in Harvey 2005: 214). Only oil
was exempt. This is a fairly blatant attempt to integrate Iraq with anglo-
phone/European economic and political interests. As such, it lends much
force to the analysis that the Bush administration is seeking to build an
economy in Iraq that is not simply pro-Western, but highly dependent
upon Western investment.

As I stated in the opening pages of the book, the privilege of writing
history lies with the strata that prosper in gaining hegemony over society
and culture. This does not mean that these strata are beyond contest or
that their counterfeit alibis for action are never exposed. On the contrary,
to repeat a point already made, culture develops from the constant interplay between force and resistance. As such there is a historical tendency
for political and cultural ruses to be exposed. Yet the strata that hold
hegemony have superior capacity to muffle criticism. In the case of critics
of the Iraq war this is usually done by trotting out the argument that the
world is a safer place without Saddam in power. This may be the case.
But it is no justification for the invasion, which was founded upon quite
a different rationale that has now been exposed as vacuous.

Cultural representation, ideology and hegemony

The culture of public opinion consists of a mixture of truths, half truths,
myths, political spin, stereotypes and unexamined prejudices. It is a rest-
less, turbulent culture in which readings that bring integrity to the whole
may be ascendant, but are never unopposed on the grounds that they
place a particular gloss on cultural reality. The discussion of the Allied
invasion of Iraq illustrates some of the difficulties involved in examining
cultural distortion through the prism of ideology. There can be little
doubt that *some* of the Allied allegations made in respect of Saddam's
regime were false: the biological and chemical weapons that he had
at his command in 2003 were not significant and the 'axis of evil' that
he occupied did not, or at least, has not yet, been verified to extend to
Al Qaeda. But other allegations were true: Saddam did commit gross
human rights violations; his regime was a destabilizing influence in the
Gulf; and he had the potential to develop a biological and chemical
weapons programme that, in time, might imperil local and Western
interests.

Ideology

Clearly, ideology involves cultural distortion that helps to legitimate a dominant political power. Yet, it is an error to present it narrowly as the application of consistently false ideas in the interests of a ruling class. *Sometimes* it comes near to being so. For example, Mao's cultural revolution in China consistently portrayed false ideas to buttress the power of the Communist Party. But even then, some of the ideas were true, notably that China needed to modernize and that Western interests threatened national security. Ideology operates principally through force and exclusion. Robert Mugabe's Zanu PF state in Zimbabwe currently imposes a single coercive vision of social, cultural, political and economic reality upon the population and uses physical force to engineer compliance. The opposition is censured and dissidence is not tolerated. The military junta that currently controls Myanmar (Burma) and that of Kim Jong-il in North Korea are flagrantly authoritarian regimes intolerant of diversity and free speech. They are attached to a monolithic model of culture which is antagonistic to opposition and resistance.

There can be no doubt that ideology is often brutally effective in achieving domination and subordination. But it is a high-risk strategy of control. For it engenders schisms, friction and opposition through blatant social exclusion and requires an effective, loyal police force and standing army to translate ideological policy into practice. Modern political cultures seldom resort to these means of rule, since they are inherently unstable. More generally, ideology exploits and develops a mixture of false and true ideas, drawn from a variety of social and cultural resources, and merges them into a cohesive reality, a practical material force, which organizes people and legitimates action. Typically this is not achieved by physical force but by cultural positioning and persuasion. That is, it is a matter of *hegemony*.

What are the differences between ideology and hegemony in shaping the context of political culture? We have touched upon this earlier in the book, but here let me say that ideology forces people to comply with policies and cultural practices on pain of moral condemnation, physical punishment or social exclusion. Hegemony persuades people that it is in their best interests to comply, but allows for resistance and opposition. Both ideology and hegemony are finally attuned to reproducing the power of dominant strata. Hoisting a national flag on your property is one of the most purely 'ideological' acts a citizen can take. Doing it voluntarily, to express personal support for national considerations, as occurred widely, for example, in the USA in the first months after 9/11, confirms the automatic, unquestioned identification of personal with national interests that hegemony seeks to turn into a 'state of nature'.

As Gramsci (1971) understood only too well, hegemony is difficult to combat because it works through the whole range of institutions in 'civil society' located between the state and the economy. Privately owned newspapers, magazines, television stations, national charities, national sporting events and the boy scout and girl guide movements are all to some extent agents of hegemony, which connect individuals to the dominant order of things by consent rather than coercion. To be sure, the legitimate use of physical force is retained by the state and administered through the judiciary, the army and the police. But the deep ordering of identification between individuals and ruling power is centred on culture in civil society. This is the real axis of authority. It is here, often at a subconscious level, that binding connections between might and right are forged. The strongest and most glamorous elements in culture are connoted with what is best for all.

Cultures are not monolithic

Cultural distortion is probably unavoidable in cultural life. There are three reasons for this. Firstly, modern culture is not monolithic. Even in cultures characterized by high levels of racial, religious and ethnic homogeneity, there will be diversity and many differences will occur. If this is the case, it follows that different positions on reality and truth must coexist and jostle with one another for ascendancy.

Secondly, cultural exchange and development depends upon representation. From semiotics we know that there is no direct correspondence between an object and the representation of the object. You might take the Union Jack or the Stars and Stripes to signify liberty, but to an Iraqi Shi'ite, illegal domination and ethnic repression are perhaps closer to the mark. The attempt to portray one cultural representation of an object in universal terms is therefore bound to generate opposition from individuals and groups who are positioned differently and recognize separate traditions of history and truth.

Thirdly, modern cultures are super-dynamic. Framing cultural processes and attributing chains of causality to them may be favoured because it gives culture a general sense of stability. However, the challenge is how to keep cultural categories in step with technological, scientific and cultural change and continuous market innovation. Just think of some of the main changes on the horizon in this century: the significant extension of life expectancy, through social policy and biotechnology, which will cause major changes in the life cycle, in particular with respect to old age and the public/private financing of dependency; the move towards global power blocs centred on North America, China, the European Community and some sort of as yet unclear federation in South East Asia, and the implications this has for the nation-state; the development of a nuclear capacity for terrorist cells and the consequences for urban-industrial relations; the increasing environmental risks and inevitable depletion of fossil fuels and the consequences for international air travel and domestic transport; the extraordinary expansion of Catholicism in Africa, Asia and Latin America and the implications this poses for Islam and other religions throughout the world. How will our cultural categories and theories keep pace with these changes?

Because modern cultures are not monolithic, change is super-dynamic and representation is fastened upon complex chains of denotation and connotation, hegemony is always provisional. That is why in modern nation-states, notions of resistance and struggle are not merely empty, rhetorical devices but possess real, practical force in the organization of political culture.

Interestingly, a separate set of issues with respect to representation and cultural distortion is raised when one turns from the work of Gramsci (1971), with its characteristic emphasis on hegemonic struggle and the constant clash of, and alliances between, interests, to the work of Walter Benjamin (2003) on the technology of cultural reproduction and cultural distortion.

Mechanical reproduction and aesthetic culture

Benjamin raises the fundamental question that representation isn't solely a matter of the relationship between the individual and the cultural object that is addressed. It is also about the *means* of representation through which this relationship occurs. *Naturalism* might seem an awkward word to use to describe looking at a painting in an art gallery. After all, the experience is culturally *organized*. Your bag is searched before you enter; uniformed guards monitor you throughout; your connection with the paintings is partly restricted by ropes that prevent you from getting too close. Yet, when all is said and done, you can stand in front of *Sunflowers* by Vincent Van Gogh and develop a 'personal' relationship with it.

But the nature of this relationship is quite different to that which you have with technological reproductions of the original in newspapers, magazines, film, television and video. These means of representation make images of the original highly accessible. Indeed, contemporary Western cultures possess the means through electronic and print media to achieve the infinite reproduction of cultural objects. This has consequences for how culture is experienced and perceived.

In Benjamin's view, the main consequence of replication is the decline of what he calls *aura*. The term 'aura' refers to the unique force that an original object possesses. For example, traditional culture was founded in automatic respect for original objects: the King or the Emperor; a statue or building symbolizing religious or national unity; a sword or a crown associated with a momentous historical event; a parchment or statement of freedom such as the Magna Carta or the Declaration of Independence. The force of these objects is enhanced by their distance from individuals. Distance here has a twin meaning. It refers to the cultural distance from the individual, in the sense of being positioned at a higher, authoritative level, and also to physical distance, in the sense that individuals had to make a journey or pilgrimage to have contact with the object. Modern culture transforms all of this. It makes representations of original objects universally available at your fingertips. This corresponds with a gathering lack of depth in cultural relationships. Widening access familiarizes us with the original object that we can 'see' through representations to 'own' through reproduction.

We live in the culture of the image. Implicit in Benjamin's proposition that replication diminishes aura is the notion that common perceptions of reality and truth have ceased to possess the authenticity that they conveyed in traditional society. The germ of this idea has been developed in various ways in the study of culture. For his part, Benjamin submitted that the decline of aura would inevitably be replaced by the domination of aesthetics. Aesthetics refers to perception by the senses and the designation of a person or object as beautiful, refined or tasteful. Every human culture has developed aesthetic criteria, codes and themes. In traditional society the figure of the monarch and religion was emplaced in an elaborate system of symbols and surrounded with rituals of meaning. Traditional culture was centred on a system of original objects that bestowed integrity upon the entire culture. The truth or falsehood of representations always referred back to the original objects that were symbolically positioned outside the systems of representation that surrounded them.

Modern culture is different. The proliferation and elaboration of systems of representation have combined to *decentre* and *fragment* culture from original objects that used to give integrity and cohesion to the whole, to many contested, relative, swiftly changing focus points. We live, to repeat, in an age of 'multiple modernities'. Aesthetics is more prominent in this state of affairs because it is a powerful device for achieving cogent representations of integrity, the visually compelling nature of which overwhelm the popular sense of fragmentation, contestation and relativism. That is why visual culture is so pronounced in everyday life. In a culture of surfaces and depthlessness, the well-concocted image 'says it all'.

In Benjamin's day, the aesthetics of the Nazi movement provided a depressingly powerful example of this. Marches, rallies, public gatherings, even sporting events like the 1936 Olympics, were drenched in light, people were regimented and ceremonies were staged as larger-than-life events. They brought all life together in a series of simple, dramatic polarized representations: Aryan versus Jew; Mother versus Whore; Folk versus Multiculture. Klaus Theweleit's wonderful study of male fantasies in the Nazi movement (1989) clearly shows how much Nazism used spectacle and sensation to create crushing images of might and right.

Western society is 'post-Fascist'. But it has learned the value of organized spectacle and staged events to generate a momentary sense of unity. The great stress that many countries and cities place upon bidding for major international sporting events like the Olympics or the World Cup, the resources allocated to international festivals, symposia and exhibitions, and the cultural importance assigned to film and television are all cases in point. We live in the culture of the image. The right image can revitalize cities, galvanize nationalism and mobilize economic, cultural and political resources. But images are not monolithic. Like all aspects of visual culture they are attached to chains of connotation through which cultural distortion can be applied, attributed and challenged.

Imaginary illusion and symbolic fiction

In Benjamin's approach, the possibility of redemption is still viable. A politics of resistance and opposition remains an option. We can decode images and, by doing so, break the sorcery that aesthetic force exerts over culture as a whole. But many postmodernist authors who have drawn on Benjamin's basic idea have not been so sanguine.

Jean Baudrillard (1983, 1987), for example, maintains that the question is no longer one of cultural confusion between reality and illusion. Rather, the question is one of the disappearance of reality itself. In contemporary culture, the notion of shared reality is so entangled with images manufactured and exchanged through the media that one can no longer disentangle it from fantasy. Slavoj Žižek (1997: 134) makes a similar point in respect of technobiology and virtual reality, which, he claims, have resulted in the 'loss of the surface which separates the inside from outside'. Yet he is less extreme than Baudrillard (1995). For example, Žižek is too much of a Balkan realist to follow Baudrillard in declaring that 'the gulf war never really took place'. He knows that it is estimated that over 100,000 Iraqis and 213 Allied forces died in the conflict (many of the latter were victims of 'friendly fire' (Associated Press News 10.1.01)). Yet he is also enough of a postmodern ironist to relish Baudrillard's decisive point: that the conflict was so one-sided, with overwhelming Allied superiority in military hardware, notably so-called 'smart bombs', that Iraqi defeat was a foregone conclusion. For Baudrillard, the Gulf War was played out as 'media spectacle' – a point of view that reinforces the proposition that contemporary culture has reached a stage in which fantasy and reality can no longer be disentangled. On this account, the Gulf War is a highly dramatic example of how the electronic images produced by society have taken over from the traditional idea of reality. Žižek does not go to these lengths. In his work, real things are recognized: time and death being prominent examples (Žižek 1997). Yet he is also receptive to the hypothesis that we are situated in a culture of the image where distinction between reality and illusion is often shallow, and where cultural artefacts have unprecedented force in establishing shared notions of symbolic order.

He distinguishes between 'imaginary illusion' and 'symbolic fiction'. The distinction is pivotal because it allows him to preserve the notion of 'reality' as a meaningful concept in contemporary culture. *Imaginary illusion* broadly supports Baudrillard's argument that cultural illusion has converged with cultural reality making it impossible to unravel the two from each other. At the heart of this is the proposition that cultural form has replaced traditional notions of external, constraining reality. The images produced by electronic media of reproduction recognize no constraints. They support and extend the symbolic order in which on-location practice plays out. So far, so Baudrillardian. But Žižek takes a realist turn in advocating that the concept of *symbolic fiction* co-exists with the *imaginary illusion* in defining how experience and perception occur in contemporary culture. By the term 'symbolic fiction' is meant the perceptual retention of recognition that the surface of reality is distinguishable from illusion. For Žižek then, unlike Baudrillard, a space still exists in media-saturated culture to enable individuals and groups to occupy and separate the imaginary illusion from that of symbolic fiction.

Exponents of postmodernism, no less than those of 'late modernity', are fond of presenting the context of contemporary culture in terms of depthlessness, pastiche, surface and appearance. This perspective has been hugely influential in Cultural Studies because it suggests that issues of aesthetics and cultural imagery are not limited to the cultural sphere, but are frontally relevant to every aspect of life. It is an expression of the textual-representational approach, in which culture is understood primarily in terms of signs, coding, representation and theming.

This position has underwritten the popularization of the concept of *cyber culture* in some quarters in Cultural Studies. The concept refers to the domination of life by the representations of digital culture. It gives a twist to the notion of embodiment by maintaining that these texts and representations achieve real material force in organizing and dominating on-location behaviour, embodiment, emplacement and context. In effect, culture is redefined as the reflection of the digital. The political consequence is that humans are presented as spellbound by the genie that modern technologies of reproduction have unwittingly permitted to escape from the bottle. This raises urgent questions of what it means to be human in the age of digital domination. But do we really live in cyber cultures? And is it a valid, or even particularly useful, way to try to encapsulate the central dynamic characteristics of contemporary culture?

Lara Croft/cyborg culture

Astrid Deuber-Mankowsky's study of the 'cyber-heroine' Lara Croft (2005) provides a case study of the cyborg culture thesis. It is a work that concentrates upon questions of cultural genre and cultural consumption over production and cultural politics. Lara Croft entered public consciousness as a PC game character in *Tomb Raider* (1996). Since then her influence has multiplied through television, fashion, cosmetics and the internet. Her image has been used to endorse bikinis, watches, mobile phones, sports wear, soft drinks, cars and daily newspapers. Deuber-Mankowsky maintains that the digital figure of Lara has 'escaped' the confines of the PC game format and the big screen (Angelina Jolie played her in the *Tomb Raider* (2001) movie) to become an autonomous presence and active material force in culture. The primary means of escape is mechanical reproduction in Benjamin's sense of the term. That is, the graphic and electronic reproduction of Lara make her ubiquitous. At the same time, following Žižek (1997), she distinguishes between imaginary illusion and symbolic fiction, and comes down on the side of the latter as a persisting real possibility in contemporary culture. At the same time she contends that the digital figure of Lara is a peculiarly potent influence in cyborg culture. Applying a variety of arguments from theories of cyborg culture and post-feminism, she portrays Lara as the ultimate dream woman. Her ample-breasted, curvaceous body makes her a magnetic object of the male gaze. But she is in no way a conventional sex object. Her independence and 'can-do' attitude make her an accessible role model for females. Lara is a digital figure that functions as a conducting fork for female narcissism, male desire and male/female voyeurism. For females she symbolizes an ideal woman, fearless, autonomous and, above all, with no need for men. For males she is an unattainable dream woman who represents a heady mix of authority and eroticism; while women transfer the frustrations of work, family and sexual relationships onto a same-sexed figure who can apparently do anything.

The argument does not stop with the cultural ubiquity of Lara. It also maintains that participation in cyborg culture transforms some aspects of audience/player behaviour into cyborg practice. According to Deuber-Mankowsky, PC game players who play the *Tomb Raider* series do not simply manipulate the digital figure of Lara, they *merge* with it in successive levels of interaction that require the player to develop progressively higher skills of game competence. The metaphor of relinquishing the human form and coalescing with the digital counterpart is deliberately chosen. The archetypal fusion between the human and the machine is accomplished in playing the game and carries over into culture (Deuber-Mankowsky 2005: 39). The merger between human and machine involves a culturally new type of possession, surrender and rapture that is erotic in nature. At the most extreme level, the audience/player is presented as *becoming Lara*. Eidos and Core Design, the companies responsible for marketing and producing the *Tomb Raider* games, reinforced this redefined eroticism by selecting the models Rhona Mitra, Vanessa Demouy and Nell McAndrew to promote the embodiment of Lara in human form. Yet they were careful to protect the independence of the digital original. The human models were allowed to be nothing more than representations of Lara, and they were restrained from appropriating or developing any iota of the original for their own purposes. The conventional relationship in which the human is prior to the representation was reversed, thus clinching the triumph of cyborg culture. Or at least that is what Deuber-Mankowsky concludes.

Is she right? She makes a powerful case that utilizes a variety of post-modernist expectations and anxieties about the contemporary balance between technology, belonging and identity, and gives them compelling shape in the example of Lara, who has indeed been culturally ubiquitous for nigh on a decade. But the proposition that Lara constitutes a qualitative cultural rupture with the past is questionable. Why is this? There are major problems with the hypothesis that Lara and the culture to which she belongs constitute a 'break' in the history of cultural distortion by enabling a truly novel merger between the digital and the human. The looseness of what is meant in experiential and cultural terms by the term 'merger' makes it troublesome to evaluate what exactly is being proposed here. PC players addicted to the *Tomb Raider* series may gain mental and sensual pleasure by progressively expanding their skill levels in order to maximize Lara's functionality. If this is the case, there may be some validity in using the term 'merger' to describe the relation between the human and the digital in this respect. But without testing the proposition empirically, there are dangers in extending it to apply to culture at large. In her 'Foreword' to Deuber-Mankowsky's book, Sue Ellen Case notes that Google reports 2,140,000 results for Lara Croft. Circumstantially, this is evidence of the considerable global popularity of the digital figure. But this is very different from assuming cultural identity between global consumers and Lara. The questions are, how far do players of the *Tomb Raider* series go to alter their physical appearance, adopt Lara's fashion, character and behaviour, and relinquish their biographical identity to *become* Lara?

There are difficulties in answering these questions *empirically*, since gaining funding to finance a meaningful cross-cultural empirical study is arguably inconceivable in the present funding climate. But even if one considers Deuber-Mankowsky's argument at the level of a *metaphor* for our times, the evidence of a significant merger between the human and the machine is quite weak. Theoretically, it is reasonable to propose that *some* players of the *Tomb Raider* series may become entranced by the game and acknowledge some kind of bodily or personality merger with Lara. But they are likely to be a statistically insignificant minority. The overwhelming majority of players and audience recognize an unbridge-able *difference* between themselves and Lara: they are real, Lara is digital.

The *Tomb Raider* series may have made a qualitative contribution to game technology by raising standards and this may have carried over into culture by turning Lara into a seductive digital force. But in principle, there is nothing new about this. A long tradition in the study of culture claims an influential relationship between the technology of cartoons, animation and popular culture. George Orwell (1940) remarked on the connection between cartoon creations in comics and Imperialism. He argued that comic strips on Sexton Blake, Tarzan, Sherlock Holmes and Billy Bunter have a motivating influence on boys' culture, shaping fashion, opinions and prejudice. The immense popularity of the Disney films in the 1940s and 1950s stimulated much commentary about the cultural effects of digital animation. Eisenstein argued that the Disney films embodied, what he called, the *protoplasmaticness* of popular culture (Leyda 1988). They were the visual representation of the popular imaginative ideal that human culture can be reorganized and transformed into different arrangements, shapes and patterns. Eisenstein believed that the Disney films stimulate popular culture by expanding and enriching the repertoire of popular imagery that can be applied by the people. More recently, Umberto Eco (1976) has commented on the influence on popular culture of the *Superman* cartoon strip and Ian Fleming's James Bond novels and the associated sequence of films. Like Lara all of this may contribute to eroding popular distinctions between illusion and reality. But the evidence for the larger proposition, that this erosion is now self-sustaining, seems to me to be flimsy.

Indeed, Deuber-Mankowsky (2005: 88–9) effectively argues against herself by reporting on flagging consumer interest in Lara following the release of the 'next generation' game built around her: *Angel of Darkness* (2003). The commercial failure of the game resulted in Eidos terminating Core Design's relationship with the *Tomb Raider* franchise. This suggests that the popular appeal of Lara was not ultimately based in her iconic status but in the appeal of the mechanical PC game in which she personalized play. Control of the game transferred to the California based software company Crystal Dynamics. If Crystal Dynamics holds power over the future of the game, it also controls the most important lever in developing Lara as a digital figure and marketing her image to consumers.

The problem facing Crystal Dynamics is not one of a digital figure dashing away from its control and exerting autonomous, motive force on popular culture. More prosaically, to begin with, it is an on-location issue. Consumers did not buy the *Angel of Darkness* in the expected numbers. The solution is to research how the digital figure of Lara is emplaced in relation to competing PC games and to determine the features of brand loyalty among long-standing game players. Once this data has been collected and interpreted the new *Tomb Raider* game will develop questions of Lara's embodiment to appeal to current market considerations. This may be expressed in a new look for the digital figure or qualitatively different capacities in her PC functionality. These are technical and commercial issues which ultimately have to do with the economic context in which Crystal Dynamics and Lara function as a business. The defining characteristic of this context is the market. It is market pressure that is forcing a major commercial rethink about the digital figure of *Lara*. This, in turn, reinforces the view that it is an error to see her as an 'autonomous' cultural presence or 'active' material force. For her autonomy and force is closely dependent upon the Core Dynamic business strategy which will be calculated by addressing and evaluating market circumstances. The company may not control all aspects of Lara's presence in popular culture. But it holds the key lever of power by monopolizing design and marketing issues.

If all of this is allowed, it seems to me that questions of *genre*, such as cultural presence and material force, are indeed a useful starting point in cultural analysis. But analysis will quickly get muddied if it fails to develop a perspective on the continuous interplay between genre, consumption, cultural politics and production. Deuber-Mankowsky's book is typical of many forms of cultural analysis today in skewing the discussion in favour of genre, consumption and cultural politics away from the subject of cultural production. No doubt, there are solid historical reasons for this. In the moment of the national-popular, Cultural Studies was very exercised to avoid the vulgar Marxist thesis that the economy *determines* culture and politics. The reaction against the notion that a given level of economic development gives you the Ford production line, while another level results in Benetton, The Body Shop and Motorola is understandable. It exposes the indefensible simplicity of treating culture as a dependent variable of economics.

But to the extent that this resulted in attributing exaggerated, autonomous influence to cultural politics in the form of resistance and opposition, and underestimating the capacity of capitalism to *learn* from cultural criticism, it boosted questions of genre, consumption and cultural politics at the expense of the issue of cultural production. If one stands the national-popular perspective on its head and considers the role of production in the development of culture, the phenomenal power of capitalism to redefine and reposition itself in relation to cultural criticism quickly becomes apparent. Viewed thus, Lara Croft looks less like an exponent of genuinely novel cyborg culture and more like a symptom of the new market formation which has evolved through this process of redefinition and repositioning production: neat capitalism.

8

Neat Capitalism

If you go to the Virgin.com website you will find a serene, positive success story of regular decade-upon-decade economic growth and accumulated social service. Virgin, you read, is not only one of 'the best respected brands in Britain', it is also 'the first global brand name of the 21st century'. Founded in 1968 by Richard Branson (see figure 8.1), the company began by offering one product: a student magazine. Branson moved into the mail order record business in 1970, and opened the first Virgin record shop above a nondescript shoe store at the lower end of Oxford Street, London in 1971. Already, the company mantra of value for money, innovation and informality, which together with 'quality' and 'brilliant customer service' are presented as the hallmark of Virgin today, was *in situ*. The Virgin record shop was marketed as an alternative, hip, consumer-friendly option to the starchy, impersonality of the big high street record chains. In the 1970s hippies and heads could hang out there and use the shop as a semi-drop-in centre. Suburbanite school kids (like me) could visit the shop and bask in the glow of being momentarily part of alternative London. The success of this business philosophy was soon apparent in the company's rapid programme of expansion.

Virgin opened The Manor recording studio near Oxford in 1972 and followed it a year later by founding Virgin Records. In 1977 it reinforced its reputation for risk-taking and cultural relevance by signing the Sex Pistols. Since then, the company has diversified into many areas of business, including planes, trains, finance, soft drinks, mobile phones, holidays, publishing, wines, radio and bridal wear. It still retains a major interest in the music business through the V2 recording label and the

Fig. 8.1 Richard Branson © TOBY MELUILLE/Reuters/CORBIS

Megastore chains. By 2002 it had created over 200 companies world-wide, employing over 25,000 people with an annual global turnover of £4 billion (US$7.2 billion). Invited to explain the phenomenal success of the Virgin group, Richard Branson cites 'quality service' and 'innova-tion'. Tellingly, he concludes that 'branding is everything' (http://www. Virgin.com/aboutVirgin/allaboutVirgin/richardreplies).

What are the characteristics of the Virgin brand? To begin with, the company aims to convey a powerful impression of personal, friendly, no-nonsense service to consumers. Branson is the public face of the company. His outlandish and colourful exploits with speedboats, trans-Atlantic/round-the-world hot air balloons and antique gliders have estab-lished the image of a maverick entrepreneur/adventurer and man of the people. Margaret Thatcher's decision in the 1980s to appoint him as a 'little tsar' briefly responsible for a nationwide anti-litter campaign in Britain, to say nothing of his high profile championing of condom use in the battle against AIDS and HIV, forged the popular link between Virgin and social conscience. It also enhanced the image of Branson as a man whose imagination is able to reach out and persuade ordi-nary people.

The highly public libel case that Virgin fought with British Airways over the so-called 'dirty tricks' campaign in 1992 was skilfully staged by Virgin as a David and Goliath battle in which Branson was portrayed as defending the right of air travellers to enjoy value for money and a fair deal. This reinforced the association between Virgin and consumer justice, and recast Branson in the role of a punchy street-campaigner ready to take on corrupt big business and triumph. Branson has described 'informality and information' as crucial to the Virgin business ethic (http://en.wikipedia.org/wiki/Richard_Branson). The company portrays itself as offering 'quality service' and 'doing good'.

There is an interesting conflation between business advantage and cultural logic here. Making a profit does not need to be justified or defended, because it is equated with 'making a difference'. Since this is automatically assumed to improve everyone's lives it must be applauded. Only a grouse would object. A resplendent and interesting hare of corporate ideology is set loose here: because Virgin 'does good' it follows as night follows day that it should be rewarded. The magnitude of its profits is not a sign of exploitation or market manipulation. On the contrary, it is hard evidence that the company has identified a popular cause and supplied it with an efficient, much needed service. The accent is upon *serving* consumers. The business model insinuates that companies run by 'suits', like the managers that control British Airways, leading financial multinationals and mobile phone corporations, conventionally hoodwink consumers. From the early policy of offering cut-price mail order records to slashing through the wasteful paraphernalia, red tape and corporate-speak of competing multinational financial Personal Equity Plans (PEPs), Virgin has positioned itself in the market as a company that robs the rich to pay the poor and offers plain speaking, common sense rather than corporate guff and gobbledegook.

'Doing good' and 'making a difference' is overlaid with an ethic of global responsibility and social conscience in respect of social injustice, third-world relief and disability rights. The brand has been used to develop humanitarian challenges to HIV and AIDS, and for the delivery of emergency aid to Iraq and the victims of the tsunami disaster in 2004. Provision for the less abled is a standard feature of the services offered by Virgin Active, Virgin Atlantic, Virgin Holidays, Virgin Megastores, Virgin Mobile, Virgin Money and Virgin Trains. The ethic of social responsibility and environmental consciousness is reinforced throughout the chain of businesses residing in the Virgin group. For example, the website for Virgin Books contains the information that the business focuses on a commissioning programme that publishes books which 'make a difference', dealing with challenging and innovative issues that 'others might not publish' and producing 'environmentally friendly' volumes, sourcing paper from 'sustainable forests'. Virgin Cosmetics is committed to 'ending animal testing' in the development of cosmetics and toiletries. Virgin Games undertakes to produce 'socially responsible gambling' and provides information and tools to guard against 'under-age access'. Virgin Travel supports 'sustainable tourism' and supplies travellers with a list of 'responsible tourist tips' such as 'switch off lights and air conditioning'; 'use water carefully'; 'don't buy souveniers made from shell, turtle shell, coral or wildlife'; and 'dress appropriately and respect local cultures'. Virgin Atlantic has developed its own 'Responsibility Policy and Strategy for Environmental Sustainability'. It recognizes the importance of minimizing the impact of its operations on local and global environments through fuel efficiency emissions and noise. In short, Virgin Aware defines the company as 'the people's champion', 'safeguarding the planet'. It lists six definitive qualities of the brand:

- Value for Money
- Good Quality
- Brilliant Customer Service
- Innovative
- Competitively Challenging
- Fun
  (http://www.Virgin.com/aware/intro.asp)

The impression of a personal, consumer friendly approach is reinforced by how the company positions itself in relation to new business opportunities. Typically, after intensive market research, it enters market sectors and targets established companies that have been assessed as presiding over inflexible, stale business cultures and presents itself as liberalizing and revitalizing them. For example, the Virgin Aware site provides a comparison table illustrating how Virgin has added value to the airline, mobile phone, financial services and train businesses (see figure 8.2).

Virgin is not alone in positioning itself in consumer culture as 'the people's champion'. Nike regards itself as selling trainers and acting as a sort of corporate health guru to 'enhance people's lives through sport and fitness'; IBM doesn't sell computers, it offers 'solutions'; Polaroid isn't just a camera, it's a 'social lubricant'; Benetton doesn't just sell clothes, it promotes social justice and HIV/AIDS awareness; Microsoft provides software and 'progressive' social values; The Body Shop is more than a cosmetics company, it cherishes 'compassion, a green environment

Industry	Convention	Virgin's response
Airline	Poor customer service, lack of innovation	Brilliant customer service and innovations such as onboard massages.
Mobile	Complicated contracts & hidden charges	One simple tariff and no hidden charges
Financial Services	Dull & incomprehensible	PEPS demystified; the innovative One account
Trains	Years of under-investment	New tilting, hi-tech trains

Fig. 8.2 Virgin added value

Source: <http://www.virgin.com/aware/customer.asp>

and human rights'; Pepsi is not a just a soft drinks company, it is a mouthpiece for youth rebellion.

Each of these companies seeks to go well beyond offering consumers a distinctive product. In addition, they aim to interpellate, or 'call forth'/ 'summon'/'hail', a particular type of consumer with a conscience about inequality, who is concerned about environmental pollution, values social justice and inclusion and favours an ethical basis to business practice.

We know from examining Cultural Studies in the moment of the National-Popular that the state interpellates through control of the law, the police, social work, education and public propaganda. For multinationals, the primary mechanisms are *marketing* and *advertising*. These businesses are not simply engaged in selling products to consumers, they are offering a *liberation culture* and *progressive lifestyle* that mirrors target groups in society. The appeal to conscience and environmental awareness is calculated to present the businesses in a progressive light and identify them with 'neat' trends in society and culture. What is going on here?

The emergence of neat capitalism

In the late 1990s and early years of the present century, several critics of popular culture started to address the issue of cultural production.

Prominent among them were Thomas Frank (1997), Naomi Klein (2001) and Richard Florida (2002). They argued that cultural critics had paid insufficient heed to what capitalism has learned from the counter-culture, environmental protection and consumer rights movements of the 1960s and 1970s. In their view, capitalism has moved into a new stage of cultural development in which branding, advertising and marketing link consumption with popular empowerment. This is not simply a question of re-tooling aesthetic codes and modernizing commercial genres. It involves a fundamental new set of dynamics in the culture of capitalism coming into play. This is rooted in a dual, ethically repositioned view of citizenship that simultaneously promotes what might be called *care for the self* and *care for the other*.

Care for the self is more or less self-explanatory. It is based on the ethical imperative to protect one's body by monitoring and applying specialized knowledge relating to diet, stress, environmental concerns and health risk analysis. Knowledge about all of these issues has massively expanded through the elaboration of the public sphere and the growth of the mass media. Through the internet, therapeutic and medical literature, a greater number of individuals are in a position to self-medicate and advise on self-medication than ever before. Care for the self is the inevitable expression of greater media representation of health awareness and risk issues. It would be wrong to infer that everyone acts upon it. Nonetheless, the responsibility to care for the self by being au fait with risk analysis is a prominent feature of contemporary consumer culture. Social awareness of it is more prominent now than it was fifty years ago. As such, its commercial importance has been recognized by the relevant sectors in the capitalist economy.

Care for the other is more intangible. It refers to the popular acknowledgement that individuals and groups are unequally positioned in relation to scarce resources. By extension, it recognizes that citizenship carries local, national and global responsibilities to increase distributive justice (sharing economic resources more equally) and social inclusion (ensuring that individuals and groups are not excluded on the grounds of gender, creed, colour or disability). These responsibilities are over and above fiscal contributions raised through systems of progressive taxation. They may involve no more than keeping abreast of how the various levels of inequality operate to intensify suffering. Equally, they may involve voluntary financial donations to recognized charities, giving labour to help those in need or working for the cause of environmental enhancement. In summary form they may be listed as referring to community relations, environmental action, health promotion, business standards, corporate governance, social justice and human rights. Care for the other is by no means universally recognized or practised in the West. Yet it provides part of the context in which citizenship practices and responsibilities are exploited and developed.

Care for the self and care for the other are part of a deeply rooted informalization process in capitalism. Informalization may be defined as the relaxation of social and personal controls in cultural interaction.

Florida's study (2002) suggests links between location, embodiment, emplacement, care for the self and the informalization of contemporary capitalism. He argues that successful work cultures encourage creativity. Creativity is boosted by a transparent system of financial reward and a business culture that encourages self-expression and innovation. The development of location factors, like relaxed dress codes in the workplace, flexible schedules and new work rules, are interpreted as the response of creative work cultures to assist empowerment and innovation. In a word, they allow people to *be themselves* in the workplace and thus liberate the potential inside themselves. Florida develops the argument by maintaining that what holds good for creative work cultures also holds good for cities and regions. The cities and regions that have prospered in the silicon and knowledge industry revolution since the 1980s have not done so merely by concentrating on their business plans. They have invested resources in enhancing public culture, developing recreational, play and entertainment space, encouraging the informalization of civic relations, actively applying social conscience in improving housing and creation and going beyond the state in acts of corporate citizenship. For Florida, the development of public culture in American cities like San Francisco, Austin, San Diego, Seattle and Boston explains why they boomed after the 1980s; the failure to develop public culture accounts for why cities like Louisville, New Orleans and Buffalo struggled. Informalization, then, is specifically identified as a cultural asset in economic development.

Informalization has also changed the context in which politics operates in popular culture. This is evident along many fronts. Mass society theory in the 1950s emphasized the compliance and docility of consumers. But the succeeding decades have witnessed an unprecedented outpouring of resistance and challenge to the context in which on-location behaviour, emplacement and embodiment are situated. Militant versions of this may be quite limited, but they are part of a general groundswell of public opinion that assigns greater prominence to social conscience and 'making a difference'. From the Live Aid, Live 8 protests at third world hunger, the disruption by anti-capitalist groups of the G8 summit

to the anti-smoking campaign, movement against environmental degradation, animal rights movement and anti-racist campaigns, fundamental
questions relating to empowerment, distributive justice and social inclusion have been raised.

It would be rash to submit that a transition into an era of consumer
empowerment has been accomplished. Nonetheless, the old idea of an
all-powerful alliance between the state and big business over the docile
'lonely crowd' of mass of consumers doesn't hold water either. Consumer resistance to capitalism has crystallized new forms of belonging
and solidarity. This is not a uniform mass movement against capitalism.
Rather it is a movement along many fronts, with unequal levels of political development and mixed types of cultural solidarity. This makes it
tricky to claim that unified political and cultural opposition to capitalism
exists. Even so, these developments have significantly changed the political and cultural context in which capitalist enterprise operates.

A striking feature of the movements of resistance, challenge and opposition in the West is their relatively non-violent nature. Instead they are
typically marked by a carnivalesque spirit in which absurdity, irony,
comedy and sarcasm are used before violence to expose conventions of
power. Business has been a target of these interventions, but it has also
learned from them. Broadly speaking, corporate capitalism has moved
from the postwar benchmark of selling consumers a mass culture lifestyle, through the creative rebellion of the 1960s, 1970s and 1980s to
the irreverence and knowing, ironical detachment of today. In the process
neat capitalism was born. The impression developed that corporate
capitalism was being played at its own game. Its hidden mechanisms of
exploitation were being made transparent, so increasing consumer choice
and correcting the dehumanization and disinformation of the system.

The meaning of neat capitalism

Frank (1997) takes the American advertising industry as a symptomatic
case. In the 1950s the industry was dominated by legendary campaign
gurus like David Ogilvy and Rosser Harris. They based their business
model on an image of American society that assumed perennial economic
growth, social conformity and cultural stability. The imagery and content
of their advertising was aimed at white, suburban, home-owning, het-
erosexual, nuclear families who enjoyed full employment and rising
prosperity. Dissent, difference, joblessness and illness did not figure in
the picture. Instead this approach was overwhelmingly dominated by

aesthetic codes and cultural material that communicated positive images of contentment, affluence and an escalator of progress that had no end to it. This view of American society was challenged by a number of academic critics of mass culture, such as David Riesman, William Whyte, J.K. Galbraith, Herbert Marcuse and Vance Packard. They emphasized the sterile regimentation of American society, public squalor in the midst of private affluence and the complacent, consumption-led introspection of mass culture.

Their arguments paralleled the rise of the counter-culture and consumer rights movement that attacked the sacred cows of affluent society, notably mindless materialism, indifference to the environment and the superficial 'feel good' ethic of consumer society. They were treated sympathetically by a new generation of 'creative rebels' in advertising, including Bill Bernbach, Howard Gossage, Jerry Della Femina and George Lois. Their work emphasized youth and incorporated social criticism and cultural disquiet. It defied the culture of conspicuous consumption celebrated by the Ogilvy–Reeves axis. For example, advertising for Volkswagen cars emphasized their durability and humble design and contrasted it pointedly with the model of planned obsolescence, extravagant design values and fuel inefficiency favoured by many of their American rivals.

Although this transformation in capitalism *began* as a move to take social and cultural criticism seriously, it developed into the emergence of a new cultural formation: neat capitalism. This is a complex social, political, cultural and economic formation that has changed the way in which popular culture operates. At its heart is the presumption that socially responsible market solutions are the most efficient way of dealing not only with economic problems, but also with social and cultural questions. This goes beyond the attempts of the creative rebels in the 1960s and 1970s to market critical lifestyles that embrace social conscience and environmental humanism. Instead 'liberation marketing' was developed which associated discerning consumption with self-actualization.

Cultivating social conscience and planetary awareness may not have been new. Cadbury, Rowntree, Sears Roebuck and Kellogg had provided precedents in the nineteenth century. But they were paternalistic models of socially aware enterprise that recognized a formal division between philanthropy and entitlement. Using humour as a device to reveal the gnomic logic of the system which still worked to contain creativity and instil obedience would never have occurred to these entrepreneurs.

Neat capitalism is different. It uses irreverence and *partnership* with the consumer as the decisive tools to expose business cant and calcified corporate humbug. At its best it startles complacency, aggravates convention and inspires consumers to embark upon progressive change. In its own way, liberation marketing draws directly on the 3 D's that cultural critics hold define late modernity: deconstruction, demythologization and demystification. It is hostile to cant and hypocrisy and it refuses to take 'no' for an answer. The accent is upon a 'can do' attitude among consumers and changing business practices built around convention, domination and waste.

The application of these principles in the construction of brand culture has displaced social interest from the traditional socialist project of transforming capitalism. For reforming capitalism from within is portrayed as a more relevant answer to the ills of the system than the socialist solution. Tacitly, the market is assumed to be the best solution to social and economic problems. This was fortified in the 1990s by the collapse of the communist alternative in Eastern Europe. With the fall of the Berlin wall, capitalism ceased to face a meaningful Cold War opponent and declared itself to be the *only* credible form of advanced urban-industrial system.

But victory over communism is not what made capitalism neat. It was the capacity of capitalism to perpetually reinvent itself not only against the challenges of socialism and communism, but also in the face of the unreformed model of traditional multinationals. The new neat capitalist corporations accentuated the requirement to listen to consumers, adopted innovative, flexible solutions to social, political and economic problems and developed ethical business practice and social conscience as primary organizational values. As Richard Branson observed, their management teams recognized that in the culture of the image 'branding is everything'. Neat capitalist corporations emphasized the fun and self-fulfilment to be had in 'doing good' and 'making a difference'. More understated is the message that adopting this business philosophy generates millions of dollars for the shareholders who back it. Neat capitalism isn't just a cultural reaction against big business and socialist solutions, it is a coherent business strategy aimed at capitalizing on the economic opportunities of the market today.

What exactly is different about these opportunities? In large part they are the product of social and cultural change. The enlargement of the public sphere, especially after the rise of satellite broadcasting and the internet, has extended and intensified media scrutiny of private and public affairs and magnified the flow of news. In the West, citizens today are probably better informed than they have ever been about social, cultural, economic, technological, medical and scientific issues. It may be legitimate to respond that this is primarily experienced as a surface awareness of globalization and culture. As much is implied by Jameson's account of 'late modernity' (1992). But the surface gloss can always be penetrated by consumers who are intent on finding out about what really drives the system. The glib, bland aspects of living in global culture can be erased to reveal the influence of more substantial ideological and material forces.

Crucial in this respect has been the parallel postwar expansion of higher education. In Western democracies, the number of young people who now experience higher education is unprecedented, with levels of participation reaching between 35 and 50 per cent in most of the leading economies. The experience of gaining a university education is now so familiar that we forget its historical importance and novelty. We can illustrate the point by briefly referring to recruitment trends in British universities since the outbreak of the Second World War. In 1939 only 3 per cent of the eligible age range was studying at university. Furthermore, these students were overwhelmingly middle/upper class, male, white and self-funded (Ainley 1994). Postwar anxieties about skilled manpower shortages and an egalitarian commitment to increase education opportunities produced a massive expansion in student numbers. In 1957/8, 97,851 full-time students were enrolled in higher education in Britain; by 1967/8 the number had more than doubled and stood at 205,195 (Beecher and Kogan 1992). Part of the stimulus behind this expansion was the Robbins Report. It recommended growth in student recruitment on the basis of four main principles: (1) to increase the competitiveness of the British economy; (2) to enhance the general 'powers of the mind'; (3) to advance learning for all those qualified by ability; and (4) to transmit common culture and common standards of citizenship.

The Education Secretary, Keith Joseph, in the first Thatcher administration successfully redefined this expansion as a feather-bedded nest which smacked of the, in his view, discredited values of the permissive society. Joseph set about applying market values to the university system. He delivered the largest ever reduction in grant income to the British higher education system. The 15 per cent cut led universities to seek to reduce student intakes by 5 per cent in order to protect the unit of resource (Scott 1995). Despite this, Thatcherism presided over a wave of expansion in student numbers. This was continued in John Major's Conservative administration and the Blair governments after 1997. In 1991, 451,000 students were enrolled in full-time higher education in Britain; seven years later the number climbed to 563,000 (Schuller 1991). Dale (2005), citing figures from the Higher Education Statistics Agency, reports that in 2001, 1,856,330 students were enrolled in full-time higher education. Moreover, the gender and racial mix of students is now far more varied than fifty years ago. Women now make up approximately 55 per cent of the student body. Students from ethnic minorities account for 13 per cent of the total.

One can argue long and hard about the effects of expansion. Although many counter-arguments might be made, the general point that a larger percentage of the general population is more literate in reading politics, culture, economics, science, technology and society is surely sound. While it can be exaggerated, it is perhaps correct to view the notion of 'active citizenship' (centred on care for the self and care for the other) as a more appropriate term to apply to consumers today than the 'mass society conformists' or 'cultural dopes' that were thought to prevail in days of yore.

Generation X and Y

Neat capitalism recognizes that these enumerated social, cultural and political changes have left an imprint on economic culture. Generation X is defined by marketing companies as citizens born between 1965 and 1980 who are characterized by a propensity for technology, scepticism to advertising claims and attraction to personal style rather than designer labels. They are estimated to constitute 17 per cent of the US population (50 million people) with consumer spending power of $125 billion per annum. Generation Y refers to people born between 1981 and 1995 (57 million of the US population). They are the largest consumer group in American history, with purchasing power of $172 billion per annum. Successful Generation Y brands are regarded as hip and popular. Heavy commercialism is deplored. Generation Y is more conscious of racial and sexual diversity. One in four members lives in a single parent household and three in four have working mothers (http://www. onpoint-marketing.com).

Neat capitalism takes the existence of Generations X and Y seriously. Specifically, it recognizes that a spirit of irreverence unites both cultures. This is frequently adopted as a direct part of advertising and marketing campaigns. Their aesthetic codes mirror populist culture in being constructed around absurdity, humour, informality and a playful disrespect for authority. But irreverence is also exploited and developed to create a political agenda that emphasizes defiance, relevance and populism.

The Body Shop

The Body Shop website list of values is typical. Even the name is populist. We all have bodies, but, of course, they are coded and themed by gender, class, race, nation and many other structural influences. The Body Shop automatically implies that we are all in the same boat: 'we' against the forces threatening the planet; 'we' against the scientists, bureaucrats, government officials and petty civil servants who gum up the works and make everyday life more fretful than it needs to be. The personal pronoun 'we' is used in an unparticularized way. It is as if the universal threats to the environment and the collective quality of life override issues of sexual, racial, regional, national and class *habitus*, coding and theming.

Not surprisingly, like Branson's Virgin companies, The Body Shop emphasizes a partnership with customers that will 'make a difference'. This is pursued around five main corporate values that are presented as defining the organization:

- Against animal testing: the rejection of testing Body Shop products and ingredients on animals on the grounds that it is 'morally and scientifically indefensible'.
- Support community trade: assistance for 'small producer communities' who supply the company with 'natural products'.
- Activate self-esteem: defining customers as 'unique' and committing the company to treating everyone as an 'individual'.
- Defend human rights: declaring that it is a universal responsibility to 'actively support those who have their rights denied to them'.
- Protect our planet: committing business to responsibility to 'protect the environment' both locally and globally.

The commitment to make a profit and expand the business is not mentioned in the list, which is strange, since it is the dynamo of the entire organization. Instead, the impression is conveyed of a company more passionately focused upon humanitarian and ethical considerations than economic and business imperatives. The activist response to human rights, animal testing and ecological issues, which have been traditionally interpreted as the responsibility of government, suggests that the state is somehow not 'making a difference'. Indeed neat capitalism reproduces the central tenet of the neo-liberal revival that only market solutions work in the long term. The market gives you private affluence and the iPod; the state gives you the internal market in the health service, the cumbersome and expensive audit culture in schools and universities, and the horrendous trail of complacency, error and passing-the-buck that failed to deal adequately with the effects of Hurricane Katrina in 2005 and temporarily turned one of the most prosperous cities in the USA, New Orleans, into a ghost town. Essential to this is the proposition that neat capitalist companies have a role of corporate governance in partnership with elected government. These companies act as sort of 'corporate citizens' representing the socially excluded and articulating public opinion. There are sound business reasons for this. Research into British consumerism indicates that 51 per cent of the public have chosen a product or a service because of an organization's socially responsible reputation (*Nottingham Trent University Grapevine* 2005: 13). Crucially, however, they are different to governments in not being elected by the electorate. Instead, they are controlled by a Chief Executive Officer, answerable to a board of shareholders, who are committed to enhancing the reputation of the organization as a socially responsible 'good neighbour'. Moreover, the decisive indicator of business success is not how the company is regarded by the public, but the size of the dividend it generates for shareholders. Neat capitalism has far from eliminated the profit motive. Rather it has repositioned it to signify social and cultural worth as well as economic value.

Of course, it would be churlish to dismiss the activities of companies like the The Body Shop and Virgin in protecting the environment, defending human rights, promoting self-esteem and delivering relief in crisis management situations as in South East Asia in the wake of the tsunami and in Kosovo, East Timor and Iraq, as merely canny business strategy. Doing something is better than doing nothing. If the examples of Richard Branson and Anita Roddick, founder of The Body Shop, can inspire ordinary people to mobilize their social conscience, devote voluntary labour or funnel financial donations to charity and relief work, more power to their elbow. But these activities aren't narrowly confined to issues of 'good citizenship'. They identify progressive values and meaningful solutions with neat capitalism. The association of marketing with 'liberation', socialism and big business with 'irrelevance' and 'history', and neat capitalism with freedom, enrichment and social solutions works at the level of *connotation*. Neat capitalism is interpellated as the fulfilment of consumer rights in that it presents itself as what you would do as a responsible citizen if you happened to gain control of a multi-million dollar business. But the business logic behind doing this is overpowering.

In a word being 'neat' helps Virgin and The Body Shop to shift more units from their shelves.

Apple

Neat capitalism defines the socially responsible market as the best tool for personal liberation and economic efficiency. In addition, it aggressively distances itself from models of bureaucratic big business that convey elitist values, formality and narrow economic values of profit and loss. Outwardly at least, neat capitalism is militantly populist. It supports innovation, free competition and consumer rights.

One of the most successful corporate examples of this in the last thirty years is Apple. Founded in 1976, the company has consistently pioneered innovative technologies and populist strategies to achieve brand distinction. The Apple Classic, the Mac II, the iMac, the titanium coated G4 powerbook and the iPod are all examples of Apple products that captured the public imagination and achieved appreciable commercial success. Less well remembered are the expensive Lisa computer which wasn't compatible with anything else on the market and the hand-held Newton Message Pad. Both products were costly to develop, were trumpeted by Apple as revolutionary breakthroughs and quickly flopped.

Apple holds less than 3 per cent of the personal computer market but it has achieved extraordinary brand loyalty. An intense and durable cult has grown up around the brand. Kahney (2004: 7) characterizes Mac users as people who are 'liberal, free thinking . . . dress well, look good and have discerning taste'. They are employed in creative industries such as music, art and design, film, the media and cultural research. Through the cultivation of a strong design philosophy, which begins from the premise that computers should be easy to use and appreciated as aesthetic objects, Apple has consistently appealed to the creativity and daring of consumers. Nowhere was this symbolized more dramatically than in the 1984 advertising campaign to announce the first Macintosh. Directed by Ridley Scott, the ad was aired in the peak slot of the 1984 American Super Bowl. Subsequently, it has become recognized as one of the first examples of 'event marketing', in which the promotion generates as much excitement and coverage as the product itself. It was one of the first ads to adopt irreverence as a central motif, for most business commentators believe that its subtext was a thinly veiled attack on Apple's major PC competitor of the day, IBM.

The ad opens with an athletic young woman, wearing bright red jogging shorts and a white Mac T-shirt being chased by security guards. She wields a sledgehammer and bursts into a dark auditorium occupied by serried ranks of shaven headed, regimented drones staring vacantly at a giant screen portraying a hectoring, hypnotic address from Big Brother. The heroine smashes the screen with the sledgehammer and a radiant burst of light engulfs the auditorium. The closing shot is accompanied by a voice-over that states: 'On January 24th, Apple Computer will release Macintosh. And you'll see why 1984 won't ever be like *1984*.' Provocatively, the Macintosh computer is never shown on screen. Consumer desire for the product is entirely generated by metaphor, auto-suggestion and connotation. The ad accomplishes the subtle transference of positive identification for the dilemma of everyman located in bureaucratic, depersonalized culture, memorably expressed in Orwell's novel, to the Macintosh, which defies the norms of big business in the knowledge and information sector.

The ad generated an unprecedented amount of interest in the Macintosh and has assumed legendary status in the history of modern advertising. What is appreciated is not only the conceit of running the ad without ever showing the product, but the subliminal and devastating attack on the implied business ethic of IBM. For of course, Big Brother represents IBM, who at the time was threatening Apple's market share of the PC market. Linzmayer (2004: 111) consolidates the point by reproducing the text of Big Brother's harangue in the 60-second version of the ad:

My friends, each of you is a single cell in the great body of the State. And today, that great body has purged itself of parasites. We have triumphed over the unprincipled dissemination of facts. The thugs and wreckers have been cast out. And the poisonous weeds of disinformation have been consigned to the dust-bin of history. Let each and every cell rejoice! For today we celebrate the first, glorious anniversary of the Information Purification Directive. We have created for the first time in all history, a garden of pure ideology, where each worker may bloom secure from the pests of confusing and contradictory truths. Our unification of Thought is a more powerful weapon than any fleet or army on Earth! We are all people. With one will. One resolve. One cause. Our enemies shall talk themselves to death. And we will bury them with their own confusion!

Thus, the mega corporations (in this case IBM) and the state are identified with dogma, creativity deficit and unapologetic manipulation.

Heroic, creative solutions spring from the companies that listen to the people and learn what is missing from ordinary lives. The future belongs to companies and people that 'make a difference'. The ad subtly connects the grey, decaying world of Soviet communism with the antiseptic, depersonalized world of Western big business. As with Virgin and The Body Shop, Apple portrays itself as the consumer's champion.

The latest iteration of this in the Apple product range is, of course, the launch and marketing of the hugely successful iPod. Originally released in 2001, this music player utilized a high speed FireWire interface for file transfer. It employed a miniaturized hard drive that made the device a quarter of the size of competing music players. The interface exploited the Apple design principle of making use as intuitive as possible. The launch was accompanied by the now famous, multi-racial, youth silhouettes series of ads. These were famous because the use of silhouettes suggested a multi-ethnic, cosmopolitan society in which everyone is an equal member of iPod-world. The iPod interfaced with iTunes the digital media player that enabled users to burn songs. In 2003 Apple launched the iTunes Music Store, which, in partnership with the 'Big 5' record companies BMG, EMI, Sony Music Entertainment, Universal and Warner, offered users over 200,000 songs to legally download at 99 cents a track. The iTunes Music Store quickly achieved market domination of the online music business. By the end of 2005 Apple had sold over 600 million tracks (*The Guardian* 3.11.05). However, the royalties and partnership fees left Apple with small change from the business. The real strategy behind the iTunes Music Store was, of course, to create a legal, cheap download service that would magnify sales of the iPod, where profit margins are much higher. The company is estimated to control 80 per cent of the music player market (*The Guardian* 3.11.05). Apple is now exploiting the philosophy of the 'digital hub' which is intended to make its computers the centre of a lifestyle network linking music (iPod/iTunes), film (iMovie), photography (iPhoto) and web access (Safari).

Neat capitalism: the basics

What are the basics of neat capitalism? It is a complex reconfiguration involving interaction between many refined codes of aesthetics, repositioned economic criteria, a revitalized business culture focusing on 'doing good' and 'making a difference', and ethical business revisions. The neat capitalist companies that I have examined seek to appropriate the aura of 'cool' from cool capitalism (McGuigan 2006) and present themselves as regular, responsible 'big citizens'. Their interpretation of corporate social responsibility and governance emphasizes a 'can do', 'hands-on' attitude to questions of social inclusion, distributive justice and empowerment. This is very reminiscent of the critique that Cultural Studies started to make in the 1960s of 'traditional' intellectuals and academics. They were portrayed as being self-referential, paying undue attention to their own systems rather than the 'real' world and failing to engage with new political and cultural realities.

Compared with what might be called traditional capitalist corporations, there are six key features of neat capitalism.

1 *Informality* Neat capitalism openly distances itself from the business culture of 'the suits'. The accent is upon self-expression, challenging convention and using irreverence to unravel dogma and humbug. 'Think Different', the successful advertising campaign that Apple ran to sell Macintosh computers in the 1990s, defines the governing self image of neat capitalism.

2 *Social conscience* Business goals are repositioned from the defining imperative of the corporation, to a means of 'doing good' and 'making a difference'. Neat capitalism acknowledges that the ethical dynamics of conventional capitalism have been responsible for human rights abuses, the exploitation of labour (especially in the developing world) and environmental degradation. It is ethically driven by issues of social conscience especially those centred around political empowerment, distributive justice and social inclusion.

3 *Innovation* Neat capitalism is smart capitalism. It makes a virtue out of a 'can do' attitude that challenges business conventions. The aim is to make products and services more simple and relevant for consumers. This involves the perpetual redefinition of business organization and outputs. Neat capitalism encourages employees and consumers to suggest ways of making their business 'do better'.

4 *Listening to consumers* Neat capitalism seeks to build a partnership with employees and consumers. Unapologetic populism defines the business culture and reinforces the differences between neat capitalism and big business. This carries over into a commitment to deliver excellent service and value for money. The implication, again, is that big business fails in each of these regards.

5 *Flexibility* Neat capitalism listens to the market. Business output is heavily influenced by design and marketing. Brand recognition is defined as a key asset. Because of this neat capitalism allocates con-

siderable resources to advertising and image management. The emphasis on listening to the market translates into flexible growth strategies. So Virgin from its base in the record retail business in the 1970s has evolved into a hydra-headed corporation serving markets in transport, financial services, soft drinks, radio and cosmetics. Similarly, Apple has achieved market domination of the internet CD download business through the itunes Music Store (which is also, of course, designed to increase sales of the iPod).

6 *Fun* Neat capitalism is anti-authoritarian, anti-elitist and anti-establishment. By identifying business with corporate citizenship neat capitalism repositions making money as an activity that answers urgent social needs. Doing good is inherently pleasurable. The business credo of neat capitalism is, *what's the point of doing anything if it isn't fun?*

There are difficulties with this business logic. There is a good deal of fun to be had in making money. But the market model is based in charging consumers more than the cost of production of a given commodity or service, and applying advertising and marketing to boost demand. The economic difference between the cost of production and these added elements is another name for 'enterprise'. The question that must be asked of Virgin, The Body Shop, Apple and the other exponents of neat capitalism is, does the enterprise discharged justify the profits accumulated? This question is obscured by a blanket marketing rhetoric that iterates that neat capitalism 'makes a difference'. To counter-balance this, we should be aware of the scale of monetary value that successful enterprise delivers. For example, the *Sunday Times Rich List 2005* (http://www.times.online.co.uk) estimated that the personal wealth of Sir Richard Branson is £3 billion; that of Dame Anita Roddick is £95 million. The *Forbes Rich List 2005* (http://www.forbes.com) estimated that Steve Jobs, Chief Executive of Apple, is worth $3.3 billion – a mere moth to the butterfly that is the richest American: Bill Gates of Microsoft, who is worth an astonishing $51 billion. Ethical business practice is one thing; socially responsible capitalism is another. But these levels of personal wealth, which at the peak rival the gross national product of some developing countries, knock common-sense notions of 'equality' and 'justice' into a cocked hat. They raise the question of whether neat capitalism changes the fundamentals of the system, or whether it is best seen as a revision to the long-standing market logic of profit maximization.

More than this, the corporations that these individuals lead incontestably have considerable power to exert greater influence upon cultural production and market cultural genre. They make great play of listening to the consumer. No doubt they do so with fidelity and sincerity. But they also generate systematically distorted genres of cultural distinction and exert active, material force over cultural consumption and cultural production. Their superior power to position and distort culture must not be obscured by the rhetoric of consumer populism that they wrap around their product range. Neat capitalism is still a system dominated by big fish. The questions of positioning, resistance and hegemony raised by traditional accounts of cultural politics have not been superseded. Rather they have been redefined and recast in a different cultural setting. This has changed the context in which genre, production, consumption and cultural politics operate. Neat capitalism may be more responsive to consumers and more attentive to the ethical dimensions of consumer practice. But it has not set consumers free. To be sure, its success has contributed to widespread scepticism that the market system can be transcended. Neat capitalism changes the agenda of resistance from overcoming capitalism to living with it and tying cultural politics to resistance and doing good within the context of the market rather than heralding a revolution in business practice.

Neat Publishing

It is tempting for students of Cultural Studies to suppose that their awareness of the various cultural processes of coding, theming and representation immunizes them from contamination. But to do so would be a delusion. Cultural expression and interplay occur in countless ways from telling jokes, writing letters, playing sports to taking photographs, fashion, dancing and making music. Although Cultural Studies is actively concerned with visual and oral traditions, the central currency for producing, exchanging and consuming ideas, information and arguments in the field are books and journal articles. It is important to be clear that the market for ideas does not exist in some privileged realm of existence that is independent of general market principles. By presenting positions in Cultural Studies through publications you engage with the marketing systems of publishing corporations that are designed not merely to provide outlets for important, worthwhile thought, but to maximize sales. Necessarily, this involves compliance with some of the devices and principles of capitalist organization that in the forum of academic life or open public debate would probably invite criticism and censure. This applies to the most basic level of issues of the copy for the blurb of books, endorsements, cover design and lay-out. But it also covers wider issues of how publishers *position* books and journals in the intellectual property market, the claims they make in advertising them and the promotional devices they employ in selling them.

In the early days of Cultural Studies, before an appreciable critical mass of undergraduate courses were established and running, in the moment of the National-Popular, the outlets for publishing were scant.

True, the work of Hoggart, Thompson and Williams was widely available. Some of their publications, such as *The Uses of Literacy* (Hoggart 1958), *The Making of the English Working Class* (Thompson 1963) and *The Long Revolution* (Williams 1965), even enjoyed a measure of popular success in that they were read beyond campus audiences and discussed in the national media. But these were writings on culture *before* Cultural Studies had begun to crystallize as a field of research and debate. Instead of being regarded as harbingers of a new approach to popular culture they could just as plausibly be classified as belonging to the deeply rooted literary tradition of dissent, in which independent-minded, liberty-loving, anti-establishment values helped to define British national consciousness.

It was not until the 1970s that publications began to appear written *in the name of* Cultural Studies. Of pivotal importance here was the cottage industry of Working Papers, established in 1972 at the Birmingham Centre for Contemporary Cultural Studies. This was a solution to an urgent, practical problem: the indifference of mainstream academic publishers to the field. This indifference might appear to be odd today given the prominence of Cultural Studies. But it did not look odd to publishers in the early 1970s, when the dimensions of the field were obscure because they were in the process of being formulated and when no undergraduate degree programmes or international research groupings existed. At this time people interested in popular culture were often employed in Departments of English, History or Sociology. They were categorized and divided by disciplinary boundaries. It was as if they were sleepers who could not be properly activated until Cultural Studies emerged as a cause célèbre. The winnowing effect on these academic boundaries produced by the cultural turn lay in the future. In the early 1970s, publishers faced difficulties in commissioning and marketing books on culture because the market was ill-shaped, uneven and diffuse.

An unintended by-product of the Birmingham Working Papers was the validation of the romantic, outlaw status of the field. Publishing typed, A4 stapled copies of 'Working Papers' and exchanging them among the cognoscenti and students new to the field suggested that Cultural Studies was exploring areas of culture and society and developing knowledge too dangerous and hot for publishers to handle. It contributed to the mystique of the Birmingham Centre as an axis of knowledge and research that was more innovative and dangerous in its treatment of questions of cultural genre, power and knowledge, popular culture and non-print technologies of cultural exchange than the established disciplines in the traditional Humanities and Social Sciences. In a word, it helped to make Cultural Studies 'neat'. Those who researched and studied it were 'neat' by association.

By way of anecdotal support for this, I remember being a research student in the Department of Sociology at the University of Leicester in the late 1970s. Although no more than an hour's drive from Birmingham, most of the Leicester staff and students had only a flimsy knowledge of the work being done at the Centre for Contemporary Cultural Studies. It relied chiefly upon reading journal articles or occasional papers published by staff and affiliates of the Centre or staff seminars with visiting lecturers. I don't think I'm misrepresenting the local native knowledge in the Department of Sociology housed in the Attenborough Tower in Leicester during this time by stating that the Centre was associated with Marxism and a vaguely subversive approach to the curriculum and pedagogy. Then, in the pre-internet age, universities were much more hermetic than they are today. At the same time, I remember sensing that something exciting and important was going on in Birmingham that made the sociological approaches that I was being exposed to in Leicester in some unparticularized way vulnerable. By the end of the 1970s this feeling was reinforced by books from Birmingham which frequently dwelt on the limitations of established sociological and literary approaches to questions of culture, knowledge and power.

Parenthetically, one should note similar traditions of mystique with respect to the rise of Cultural Studies in other countries. The redoubtable Meaghan Morris (2006) recounts working in Australia in the early 1980s as a part-time lecturer writing on an Olivetti manual typewriter for small magazines and journals aimed primarily at Australian readers. Her reminiscences powerfully convey not only the sense of writing about subjects that were on the boundaries of established disciplines, but also the situation of being physically positioned on the margins in part-time labour for raggle-taggle publishing outlets. Even today the idea of developing Cultural Studies against the grain of the established culture in universities, publishing houses and the media is fundamental to the self-image of people working in the field. But of course, it is much harder to associate mystique with the subject since it has become well established in the university curriculum, the commissioning lists of academic publishing houses and the address books of radio and TV producers seeking pundits to contribute to media broadcasts.

To be sure, as early as the mid-1970s, academic publishers were becoming interested in building book-lists around Cultural Studies. Hutchinson was the main publisher of book collections of the

Birmingham Working Papers and original works. They marketed them as cutting-edge books that contributed to the birth of a new critical field of knowledge. The anti-establishment character of Cultural Studies was prominently stressed. This was a fair reflection of the work emerging from Birmingham which located culture in the context of the crisis of Western capitalism. This crisis was defined in terms of the contradictions of the welfare state, the marginalization of multi-ethnic groups and the politics of class domination.

The positioning of Cultural Studies as an intellectual and moral response to the crisis of capitalism was a significant factor in explaining its popular appeal. Not surprisingly, the data for most of this work came from Britain. A major difference between Cultural Studies publishing at this time and later was that publishers were willing to publish book-length works which dealt with national issues: Willis's *Learning To Labour* (1977), Hall et al.'s *Policing the Crisis* (1978) and Gilroy's *There Ain't No Black In The Union Jack* (1987). This reflected the pioneering status of these writers who were researching and publishing before the field of Cultural Studies had been fully born. By the mid-1990s, publishers were grumbling that books dealing with national conditions did not 'travel well'. The only exception was the USA where the size of the domestic market ensured adequate demand for book-length works on American cultural issues. British publishers defined the anglophone world as their 'domestic' market. Consequently, British, Australian, Scandinavian and Asian authors in the field were encouraged to publish books that focused on positions and principles rather than empirical data. The result was the establishment of a textual environment in Cultural Studies which focused on 'Culture' as opposed to specific cultures and theory rather than empirical research. This was modified somewhat by the development of journals in the field in which empirical work dealing with national questions was often featured. Typically, however, journal articles carried less status than book length works. A peculiarity of the field, then, is that most of the canonic texts in Cultural Studies address large and often abstract questions of culture such as globalization, trans-nationality, hybridity, post-identity, cultural rhetoric and codes of representation, but lack a corresponding commitment to systematic empirical research.

Cultural Studies and the anti-establishment

Why was Cultural Studies regarded as producing more relevant knowledge than the established disciplines? In the moment of the National-

Popular it was the readiness of writers in the field to address ordinary life and marginalized cultures that made it significant. As the media widened access to representations of working-class and multi-ethnic life, Cultural Studies provided a battery of supporting concepts and theoretical approaches to read popular culture. This was particularly significant at a juncture in which many traditional forms of working-class life were disappearing and the effects of globalization were producing a crisis in the Keynesian version of capitalism built around a partnership between the state, business and the trade unions.

However, it wasn't just a question of being refreshingly alive to popular culture and its relation to politics. Cultural Studies also pointed to new ways of understanding culture, theming and representation. The English translation of Roland Barthes's exciting experiments in semiotics (1957) suggested a new, more objective way of conducting literary studies, investigating culture and decoding media representations. Later, under the influence of post-structuralism, interest in the ambiguity of meaning and the creative role of the reader stimulated work on cultural genre and cultural consumption that radically questioned traditional approaches to authorship, identity and representation.

In Britain, perhaps the most notable example was the Department of English in Cardiff University, which diversified into Journalism and Communication much earlier than other departments in the same discipline. Terence Hawkes eventually proceeded to edit the *New Accents* series for Methuen and, later, Routledge at the end of the 1970s. Issues of class, subculture, gender and race were implicit throughout, but seldom directly addressed. Instead, the emphasis was on new ways of reading culture, especially in relation to questions of the widening of access associated with changes in education and new technologies of representation. Typical titles in the series include *Critical Practice, Orality and Literacy, Deconstruction, Dialogism, Translation Studies* and *Reading Television*.

Along with journals like *Screen, Ideology and Consciousness* and *m/f*, the *New Accents* series provided a counterpoint to the moment of the National-Popular and reflected the growing ascendance of the Textual-Representational moment in the organization of Cultural Studies. This work expanded the influence of continental traditions of post-structuralist thought, textual and discourse analysis in the study of culture. It interpreted and applied the work of writers like Saussure, Barthes, Lacan, Derrida, Lyotard and Foucault for an anglophone audience. Books like Coward and Ellis's *Language and Materialism* (1977), Sturrock's *Structuralism and Since* (1979) and Culler's *The Pursuit of Signs* (1981) synthesized this material and suggested a challenging way of reading culture based in textual methodologies and the close analysis of representation.

This approach was less transparently political than the Birmingham position in the sense of being unaligned with an interventionist form of left-wing politics. Conversely, by radically questioning all meaning, and raising the profile of emotion, desire and fantasy in cultural, sexual and political thought, it contributed significantly to an adventurous critical front in Cultural Studies which concentrated upon the textual and representational organization of meaning. Ultimately, this led to the emergence of radical scepticism about identity and nudged critical analysis in the direction of the deconstruction of meaning. Inevitably, this in turn raised deeply political questions about the location and practice of power and knowledge in organizing the popular sense of individuality, *habitus* and political solidarity. On the other hand, at the levels of strategy and policy, it failed to yield a coherent, tenable alternative to capitalism.

The result was the dispersal of political interests in Cultural Studies along many fronts. The *Critical Idioms* series, edited for Routledge by John Drakakis of the University of Stirling, reinforced this trend with titles on *Narrative, Discourse, Magic(al) Realism, Intertextuality, Parody* and *Genre*. The challenges that this presented to traditional approaches to studying culture were particularly attractive to the generation of younger readers. Some of the main intellectual influences, such as Michel Foucault, Jacques Lacan and Jacques Derrida, were celebrated as producing a revolution in how power, knowledge, language, identity and culture were studied and understood.

At the risk of labouring the point, the various interventions from Birmingham, Cardiff and Stirling were so strongly associated with neat publishing because they broke with the inertia and hail-fellow-well-met heartiness that characterized so much of the academic establishment and took popular culture seriously. In addition, Cultural Studies was linked with a whiff of scandal which did no harm in cultivating its neat status, especially among students. Nowhere was this symbolized more aptly than in 1992 when Cambridge University announced its intention to confer an honorary degree upon the controversial French philosopher Jacques Derrida. The decision was publicly attacked in a letter written by conservative philosophers to *The Times* which accused Derrida of a lack of clarity and rigour and alleged that his method of deconstruction relied on 'gimmicks'. Similarly, dons in the Cambridge English Department deplored the initiative from the University on the grounds that Derrida's methods trivialized the study of English. The controversy spilled over by association into fields that displayed the influence of Derrida's philosophy, such as Cultural Studies. Cultural Studies came to symbolize not a lack of rigour, but a new way of analysing culture that addressed popular culture in interesting, pertinent and unpatronizing ways.

The Urbana-Champaign conferences

The explosion of courses in Culture, Media and Communication and the so-called 'cultural turn' in the social sciences after the 1980s transformed the terms of trade in which Cultural Studies operated. It was not just a question of new degrees in Cultural Studies being introduced virtually over night. The link between neat and Cultural Studies was reinforced. Crucial in these respects were two international conferences (and the publications that sprang from them), held at the University of Illinois in Urbana-Champaign, in which Stuart Hall's American student Larry Grossberg was a central figure.

The first conference was held in 1983 although the conference proceedings that emerged from it were not published in book form until 1988 (Nelson and Grossberg 1988). The long lead time between the conference and the publication of the book symbolized the uncertainty about the nature of the field. The conference and the book both had a peculiar, provisional quality about them. They displayed an obvious hesitancy about what Cultural Studies constituted and how it is positioned in relation to the established disciplines. The book more closely resembled an edited collection of conference proceedings than a christening for the birth of a new area of study. Its anti-establishment position was signalled by a close identification with Marxism, rather than the claim of novel theoretical and methodological approaches to popular culture. The resulting book addressed the rather hackneyed Marxist theme that culture is inseparable from social, economic and political relations. Although the subject of culture was privileged, the Marxist backcloth made Cultural Studies look like an appendix of critical Sociology and Criminology rather than a credible, independent emerging field.

The same could not be said of the second conference held at the same venue in April 1990. First of all, Marxism was replaced by a more ecumenical approach to cultural theory, embracing feminism, the history of knowledge, ethnography, race and ethnic studies, colonialism and post-colonialism. The accent was upon the inclusiveness and theoretical diversity of Cultural Studies.

Secondly, this approach carried over into an expanded definition of the field. There is confidence, even exuberance, about the distinctive and novel contribution of Cultural Studies. This was apparent in the book from the conference that emerged two years later (Grossberg, Nelson and Treichler 1992). The virtues of Cultural Studies are no longer portrayed in terms of taking ordinary life and marginalized culture seriously or insisting that culture is political. To be sure, these remain part of the ethos of Cultural Studies, but the emphasis in 1990 is much more upon mapping the field and differentiating approaches to it. As Hartley (2003: 162) rightly notes, the subjects listed in the 'Users' Guide' amount to a syllabus for Cultural Studies: the history of cultural studies; gender and sexuality; nationhood and national identity; colonialism and postcolonialism; race and ethnicity; popular culture and its audiences; identity politics; pedagogy; the politics of aesthetics; culture and its institutions; ethnography and cultural studies; the politics of disciplinarity; discourse and textuality; science, culture and the ecosystem; rereading history; and global culture in a postmodern age. The 1990 conference continued the association between Cultural Studies and neat. But it introduced a new note of professionalization in the subject. This was conveyed through the recognition of three theoretical and practical distinctive concerns facing the field.

1   *Globalization*   The dimensions of Cultural Studies were now recognized to be *global*. National conditions were recognized to vary and to consist of some specificities. But national cultures were now frontally addressed as situated in global contexts. In particular the place of non-Western cultures and their positioning within Western traditions, and their assimilation of Western traditions, were prominently stressed.

2   *Post-Marxism*   Marxism was no longer presented as the theoretical tradition which best unified culture, economics, politics and society. On the contrary, a variety of theoretical positions were recognized, including feminism, postcolonialism, post-structuralism and discourse analysis. Questions of cultural genre were given more prominence than had been the case in the 1983 conference, especially with respect to issues of cultural aesthetics. This suggested that the subject of cultural genre could be studied independently of production, consumption and cultural politics.

3   *Deconstruction, demythologization and demystification*   A more diversified form of cultural politics was displayed in the volume. Cornell West (1992) distilled this in his identification of Cultural Studies with deconstruction, demythologization and demystification. When Marxism dominated the fledgling area of Cultural Studies it

was assumed that the field would make a constructive contribution to building socialism. This remained a tacit assumption of the 1990 conference. But it was clear that the Cultural Studies concept of socialism was now to be regarded as a house with many rooms. These included textual analysis, discourse analysis, feminism, post-feminism, postcolonialism, postmodernism and queer theory. All of these positions contributed to the deconstruction, demythologization and demystification of cultural categories and forms. However, they differed markedly in points of theoretical stance and political emphasis. The absence of unity, and clear principles upon which solidarity could be constructed, was already contributing to a revival of interest around issues of cultural genre and identity politics. In addition it weakened the Marxist emphasis upon the centrality of class.

The 1990 conference, and the book that followed it, exploited and reinforced the growing conviction among publishers that Cultural Studies was an intellectual force to be reckoned with and presented attractive investment opportunities. Suddenly, the lock-gates that had been bolted against the subject were opened. Routledge, Duke University Press, Minnesota University Press and Sage joined Hutchinson (which eventually went out of business) as major publishers of Cultural Studies. Not only books, but a flurry of new journals was launched, the most important of which were *Cultural Studies, Angelika, Parallax*, the *International Journal of Cultural Policy*, the *European Journal of Cultural Policy*, the *International Journal of Cultural Studies* and the *European Journal of Cultural Studies*. This was a world away from the days when secretaries in Birmingham stapled typed sheets of A4 and mailed them to subscribers. Cultural Studies was now the main piston driving the so-called *cultural turn*, which seemed to be producing exciting new challenges and opportunities for the study of culture.

Routledge

Unusually, I was able to observe at first hand the attempt to brand Routledge both as a leading publisher of Cultural Studies and as a neat capitalist publishing corporation. For eight years, between 1986 and 1994 I worked as a full-time book editor, based at the New Fetter Lane, London office of the company. My job title was Senior Editor in Sociology. The company I joined in 1986 was in fact Associated Book

Publishers (ABP). This British aristocratic, family company controlled a variety of imprints producing academic book titles in the Humanities, Social Sciences and Law: Methuen, Tavistock, Spon, Croom-Helm, Routledge and Kegan Paul, Arkana, Pandora and Sweet & Maxwell. Each imprint maintained a distinctive publishing identity within the ABP structure. The directors of each were accountable to the ABP board but enjoyed considerable autonomy in exploiting and developing their individual brands. The business style was rather traditional, albeit with welcome concessions to feminism and gay and lesbian identities (but not colonialism – in my memory the ABP personnel were overwhelmingly white and I hazard the view that this remains the case in Western academic publishing). Ere long, academic publishing had been a gentleman's occupation and ABP still reflected that atmosphere. Yet, in fact, women were the majority among the editors, marketing and production components in the ABP group. Perhaps this was reflected in a company ethos of strong commitment to author care, cultivating dedicated editors and producing books of academic excellence that would appeal throughout the anglophone world. Conversely, perhaps it also reflected the relatively low pay offered by management to editors, marketing and book production personnel. Be that as it may, commercial considerations were, of course, apparent in the commissioning, production and marketing process, but they were underplayed in favour of an ethical imperative based on providing service to the academic community.

In 1987 ABP was acquired by the Canadian business conglomerate International Thomson (IT). For IT, the jewel in the crown was the law publisher, Sweet & Maxwell. This was rapidly divested from the remainder of the group. Among staff in the other ABP companies serving the Humanities, Social Sciences and Trade (drama, biography), the common view was that IT had a hazy idea of the nature of its Humanities and Social Sciences business purchase, but was prepared to give them a go at proving themselves as viable commercial concerns.

Follwing Branson's edict that 'the brand is everything', IT immediately encouraged rationalization of the old ABP brands. A new company called Routledge was created, on the grounds that the RKP brand possessed greatest global brand recognition. The object was to establish the old ABP group as a coherent brand in a marketplace that was recognized to be both crowded and competitive. The individual publishing traditions of the lists and the differences between them were secondary to establishing a big, bright, brand image that would symbolize status, excellence and vitality. What did brand names like Methuen and Tavistock and associated niche markets mean to IT? Their finance and accounting 'experts' based in Toronto and London were chiefly concerned with maximizing the bottom line, i.e. increasing profit margins. ABP brands like Methuen, with an extensive drama and flourishing trade list, were sold. The lucrative *iChing* title from the RKP backlist, and the Arkana (Mind, Body and Spirit) and Pandora (Feminism and Women's Studies) lists were sold. The 'core' concern of the new Routledge group was defined as higher education publishing for the Humanities and Social Sciences. The usual commitments were made about the importance of 'the business' to IT. Yet these commitments were a triumph of internal corporate public relations over common sense, since for most people who worked in the company, it was as plain as a pikestaff that IT had no doctrinal commitment to Routledge but would support the company only so long as the rate of return on investment warranted it. Thereafter, those in Toronto and London responsible for looking after the Thomson business would have to make the proverbial 'difficult' business decisions. But that is to anticipate matters.

After some colourful and eventful boardroom jockeying, David Croom, the co-founder of the old Croom-Helm imprint, was appointed as Managing Director of Routledge. Croom cultivated an informal style of management based upon his sales experience in Croom-Helm. It valued the importance of getting results over respecting old-fashioned publishing industry protocol or passively servicing the academic community. The accent in commissioning was placed upon titles that would be widely adopted in undergraduate degree programmes and academic research groups. This increased the significance of marketing since commissioning decisions depended less on editorial hunches or reader's reports and more on course numbers and module outlines. Commissioning remained an art. In the early 1990s one of the largest growth areas in book sales was on the subject of postmodernism, for which hardly any course outlines existed at the time. At the same time, more emphasis was placed upon the hard 'objective' data supplied by market research and student numbers. Slowly, the idea of building a book by finding the common denominators in course outlines rather than following the convictions of authors and editors began to be favoured. Editors ceased to be valued for the number of titles that they signed each year. The projected turnover on signings became the key.

Croom reorganized the ABP companies into four groups called rather unimaginatively Group 1, Group 2, Group 3 and Group 4. Group 1 concentrated on the so-called hard social sciences, such as Economics, Business and Political Science. Group 2 (in which I was located) focused on the 'soft' social sciences – Sociology, Psychology, Social Policy, Criminology and Women's Studies. Group 3 focused on the Humanities – English, History, Philosophy and Cultural Studies. Group 4 was the Reference division. The New York office was responsible for developing its own commissioning programme from US-based authors and distributing and marketing the titles imported from London.

As one would expect of the model of neat capitalism, the Routledge management style was based upon informality and a new partnership between editorial and marketing staff. One of the obvious features of the new Routledge was that marketing staff were given much greater authority in establishing the brand and influencing the pattern of commissioning. This reflected a new appreciation of the commercial worth of branding in a crowded marketplace. To some extent, the excellent quality of the Routledge backlist could be relied upon to attract authors and readers. But the design of the books and the ethos of the company were now recognized as crucial in the academic positioning and point of sale dynamic of the new company.

One feature of this was employment of the brand consultancy Newell and Sorrell to provide a distinctive look to the Routledge book list and company ethos. Many of the old ABP books were classics by world class academic writers like Wittgenstein, Popper, Max Weber, Emile Durkheim, Merleau-Ponty, David Bohm, Lévi Strauss, Konrad Lorenz, Mary Douglas, Marshall McLuhan, Immanuel Kant, Bronislaw Malinowski, Martin Buber, F.A. Hayek and Frances Yates. Newell and Sorrell's strength lay in designing and repositioning visual identity. They initiated a redesign of ABP book jackets that introduced a new colophon for the book list and the distinctive black spine (see figure 9.1). The new design was intended to make Routledge books dominate the shelves and display counters of bookshops and establish the new brand in the mind of the public. The company mission statement was redefined to combine strong market appeal with academic excellence and author care.

Routledge is a particularly interesting case in Cultural Studies publishing because it exploited its list-building in the field at a moment when it was redefining itself as the neat successor to the old ABP brands. Together with Minnesota University and Duke University Presses it played a leading role in championing Cultural Studies in the 1980s and 1990s. It still publishes what is arguably the most prestigious journal in the field, *Cultural Studies*. In addition it published the first widely adopted textbook in the anglophone market (Grossberg, Nelson and Treichler 1992).

Fig. 9.1   Routledge logo on spine

Routledge didn't just *publish* Cultural Studies, it *promoted* it partly as a way of branding the 'relevance' of the new company in the academic market. Cultural Studies at Routledge sought to be more exuberant and daring than any rival list within the company. Nowhere was this more apparent than in the commissioning programme developed in the New York office. In an interview with Jeffrey Williams, the Vice President and Publishing Director, Bill Germano, was credited with 'forging' the publishing field of Cultural Studies. When Germano was 'ousted' from

Routledge in 2005, he was described in a leading academic American publication as 'a key figure' in the rise of Cultural Studies (*Chronicle of Higher Education* 15.09.05). Germano's commissioning style paralleled the emphasis in Cultural Studies upon marginalized cultures, the impasse of stuffy traditional approaches to academic enquiry and the value of a free inquisitive spirit. As he put it:

> I want to keep myself as open as possible to all sorts of inquiries from all sorts of folks. A great idea can be any place. (Williams 1998: 3)

This translated into an adventurous, non-conventional commissioning style that sometimes provoked critics to maintain that Routledge deliberately published books with shock value in order to grab market share. Titles, like Dubin's *Arresting Images* (1994), which examined censorship in the visual arts, Goldburg's *Reclaiming Sodomy* (1994) and Garber's *Vested Interests* (1997), which dealt with the cultural anxieties around cross-dressing, are frequently cited in this regard.

Germano's response is reminiscent of the standard defence of Cultural Studies in relation to the exploration of popular culture, namely that serious investigative enquiry must be inquisitive about every aspect of human life and that it is high time to break many traditional boundaries down:

> Marjorie Garber's *Vested Interests* is a brilliant book. If one wishes to find cross-dressing unsavoury, then one may wish to avert one's eyes. And that's a reader's choice, but I think there's an enormous market for brilliantly done work in cultural studies . . . I don't think the distinction between traditional scholarship and 'cutting edge' or advanced new scholarship should be pressed as inexorably as it often is. (Williams 1998: 9–10)

But this deals with the question with kid gloves. The real issue is why Germano elected to publish a book on the subject, which he well knew many traditional readers would find unsavoury. The point is not simply that Garber's book is first rate. It is also that publishing it reinforced Routledge's image of tackling 'front line' material and refined its market image as a publishing brand willing to address 'dangerous' subjects. At a time when Cultural Studies insisted that nothing is sacred, this was a handy asset in list-building.

Paradoxically, it became an impediment once a canon in undergraduate Cultural Studies was established. Why buy books on cross-dressing and censorship in the visual arts when core modules in Cultural, Media and Communication Studies were organized around the study of a staple set of core theories and key institutions? By the mid-1990s many rival academic publishers openly dismissed the Routledge Cultural Studies list as 'trendy' and sought to develop undergraduate teaching texts that would possess high adoption value in the field.

Nonetheless, Routledge provides a powerful example of how a cultural producer can seize a cultural genre and package it to promote 'neat' associations in cultural consumption even among consumers who are professionally sceptical of the whole paraphernalia of 'marketing' and 'branding'. The link between Routledge and bold, adventurous publishing was skilfully developed and exploited. Routledge succeeded in applying the marketing and branding techniques that many Cultural Studies authors deplored on professional grounds, and repositioned them as providing a *service* to the field. Following the precedent of Virgin, The Body Shop and Apple, the new Routledge justified its business as 'making a difference' and 'doing good'. That this exercise was only tolerated by IT as long as the book business returned an acceptable profit was decorously presented by Routledge management in mid-town Manhattan and New Fetter Lane as being beside the point. Finding and promoting those 'great ideas' that can come from 'any place' was the outward expression of what the business was about. It need hardly be added that this was very much in keeping with the populist credo of the Cultural Studies of the day.

What is obscured is that Routledge editors involved in commissioning books on Cultural Studies on both sides of the Atlantic were not primarily encouraged to cultivate *unknown* lecturers or works from repressed subcultures. Instead they concentrated their commissioning resources on the proverbial 'big names' or topics that would seize the imagination of consumers in the Cultural Studies market. The dynamic in the commissioning process was not driven by some philanthropic ideal of liberating ideas and arguments from marginalized or repressed cultures or giving a platform to their representatives. It was about taking a calculated risk to publish books that established and emerging markets in the field would recognize as worth buying in bulk. However, accessible, relevant and adventurous the Routledge book programme was presented as being, it was only tolerated by IT so long as it achieved an acceptable profit. When the judgement was made that the profits were not acceptable, the company was sold to Taylor & Francis. In a word, market criteria *prevailed* over the outward culture of neat capitalist publishing.

What comes through most powerfully in considering neat publishing, and Routledge as an exemplar of the genre, is how much cultural production and consumption, even in fields that are culturally critical and reflexive, assume an *industrial* model of exchange. The brand is designed firstly to define the product but secondly, and crucially, to seduce consumers. Marketing works partly by informing consumers, but also, and again crucially, by presenting products in the best possible light. It seeks to produce identity for discourse markets. Just because this identity involves consumers that are likely to be au fait with processes of 'interpellation', 'coding', 'theming' and 'ideology' doesn't mean that these forces cease to be active. On the contrary, one might venture that these processes are *most* effective when they are marshalled and consumed in the spirit of *critical* activity, since criticism assumes a type of knowledge that renders their effects transparent through the mere act of criticism.

Conclusion: The 'Long March' of the Cultural Imaginary

The shifting horizons of Cultural Studies are strengths since it means that the field is sensitive to change. But they can also be a source of exasperation. There is the question of the misuse of cultural neat. Acknowledging and supporting difference and resistance is one thing. Seeing it everywhere, from subcultural style to youth rebellion, is too much. Meaghan Morris (1996) is surely right to be scathing about this formula by describing it dismissively as the 'banality in Cultural Studies'. The implication of her remark is that those involved in the field must learn to apply discretion: not all cultural forms or practices are of equivalent status or value.

Many people involved in Cultural Studies find this hard to accept. People have *theological* difficulties in attributing greater significance to some types of culture over others. It goes back to the critique of authoritarian and establishment positions on culture, which was so inspirational in the origins of the field. To counteract this we must remember that Cultural Studies is situated within relations of power. The *context* of scarcity in which we operate as readers, teachers and writers is based on profound inequalities in the balance of power between individuals and groups. Because we are positioned differently in relation to scarcity it is necessary to acknowledge not only that sliding scales of power ratios apply between individuals and groups, but also that this translates into important differentials in cultural significance. There is no doubt that the culture of blogging sites among sports fans and film fans is important in the eyes of the individuals and groups who participate in them. But the importance of their activities to common culture is not as significant as, say, the values of the neo-liberal executive circle affixed to the Nixon White House whose influence has remarkably extended into the Presidential administrations of George W. Bush. They constitute a crucial subcultural formation in understanding American and global culture, economy and politics over the last thirty years. One might have reservations about the outlook, values and policies of men like Donald Rumsfeld, Dick Cheney, Richard Armitage and Paul Wolfowitz, but anyone seriously interested in Cultural Studies must allow that their politics has left a decisive stamp on American and global culture.

There is something to be said in favour of honouring the intrinsic importance of all cultural form and practice. But *realpolitik* applies to culture as to all areas of human life. Some types of culture have greater influence upon context and therefore the common culture in which individuals and groups operate than others. The time has passed for students of Cultural Studies to feel inhibited in saying so. Indeed, one important task facing Cultural Studies in the next two decades is to move away from a focus on the intrinsic character of cultural genres and the process of cultural consumption to a more sophisticated understanding of the relationships between cultural production, cultural politics and the interface between national and global power elites.

This suggests that some features of the National-Popular moment should be revived. A revised approach must insist on the relevance of multiple modernities and the shifting balance of power between nation-states and global forces, rather than seeking to rehabilitate the ideas of the centrality of the class struggle or that the national-popular is the focus for political activity. The old emphasis in the National-Popular moment in situating what I have called on-location practice, embodiment and emplacement in the *context* of political economy is surely of some significance in establishing Cultural Studies on the next footing in its development.

In addition, the moment of Governmentality/Policy in Cultural Studies raises tricky issues relating to the positive contribution of Cultural Studies to the regeneration of culture and society. The 3 D's of deconstruction, demythologization and demystification offer paltry comfort to those traditionally minded left-wing writers on culture who want to build a new Jerusalem out of anti-racism, anti-sexism and anti-elitism. This is because the 3 D's are conceived as axial processes in Cultural Studies. The conclusions that they draw are themselves regarded as *positioned* and *provisional*. Through cultural interplay between individuals and groups, cultural positions will be revised and *re-positioned* in time. And there is no end to this process. No higher ground from cultural interplay and challenge exists or is possible. Deconstruction, demythologization and demystification are fated to occur *in perpetuity*.

This raises huge challenges in what I have called the fourth 'moment' in Cultural Studies, the moment of Governmentality/Policy. Most of the safe bets in Cultural Policy are concentrated in questions on the *means* of cultural inclusion rather than the *ends* of cultural policy. Few would object to respect for religious, sexual and subcultural difference, or legal and technical provisions to enhance equality and tolerance; but objections are frequently raised when policies of positive discrimination are seen to allocate greater resources to one group in society over another. The rhetoric of modern democracies insists that we are all in it together. But when we feel that the cake of public resources to which we all contribute is divided unequally, allegations of favouritism, prejudice and cronyism emerge with unnerving despatch.

How can this problem be squared with the task of making empowerment, social inclusion and distributive justice more than empty words? Two rather familiar, dare one say 'hackneyed', approaches have been applied to deal with the question: state and market solutions. Both are flawed because they misunderstand the character of the cultural imaginary and its relation to the path of common cultural and political development.

The market solution

Traditionally, the market solution applied a laissez-faire or 'let it be' perspective to culture. This involved minimum state regulation of national markets and limited multilateral agreements between states. Following Adam Smith's doctrine of 'the invisible hand' in economics it was maintained that through the pursuit of individual ends, solutions 'naturally' emerge that benefit all. While the role of regulation has become better appreciated, the idea that the market is the most efficient and impartial decision-making unit in human affairs is still at the core of neo-liberal thought. Cultural policy is increasingly formulated and applied on the principle of the *economic value* of investment and resource allocation (McGuigan 2004).

In contrast, neat capitalism offers a more complex perspective on cultural relations. Markets are associated with benefits, but costs are also recognized. In particular, markets built around high levels of inequality are regarded as problematic since the stakes are held to be rigged in favour of the powerful. Neat capitalism holds a notion of corporate governance upon which the responsibility of successful corporations to 'make a difference' is accentuated. Making a difference may be defined in various ways. Generally it is practised in respect of correcting market inequalities, promoting social inclusion, protecting the environment and responding to mass disasters such as the tsunami in South East Asia in 2004 or the North Pakistan/Kashmir earthquake of 2005. Typically, corporate governance is based on a concept of cultural representation since corporations present themselves as acting on behalf of the responsible citizen. The publicity aspects for the corporation and their leaders in acting thus are generally downplayed. Instead neat capitalist corporations generally present themselves as supplementing government strategy by offering a more flexible and sensitive response to social, cultural and economic questions uncluttered by red tape and other forms of bureaucratic protocol.

Neat capitalism is an expression of cultural populism. But in promoting a refreshing 'can do', informal attitude to issues of national and global interest it seriously distorts levels of economic and political inequality. In so far as the notion of corporate governance conveys the idea that corporations are 'big citizens' it draws a false analogy between business and citizens. Corporations are not like citizens. Their economic power, political influence and capacity to shape cultural genres make them different sorts of players in culture and the economy. In attacking rigged economies, neat capitalist companies are really undermining a particular *style* of capitalist system rather than abandoning the principle of economic inequality per se. Neat capitalist corporations still strive to maximize profit margins and achieve a quasi-monopolistic position in the markets in which they are situated. They may employ many types of cultural rhetoric such as giving the consumer a fair deal or getting away from stuffy business practices, but they remain geared up to appropriating surplus value from consumer culture. In a word: the old dog has learned new tricks, but it has not changed its spots!

The state solution

A major response to the neo-liberal revival of the late 1970s is the reaffirmation by the state of the principle that culture is a primary resource in economic development and social integration (DCMS 2000; Mercer

2002). The role of the state in defending and enhancing culture in ways that are distinct from those of multinational corporations, social movements and interest groups is recognized.

Conversely, hand in hand with the acknowledgement of the civic importance of culture is growing cynicism about the political engagement of the electorate. This raises real difficulties for the relationship between representational politics and cultural populism. The strategies of spin and spoon-feeding that governments have adopted to explain policies to voters have produced widespread disquiet about the health of democracy. For example, the attempts of Tony Blair to justify the invasion of Iraq, the enhancement of policing powers to detain criminal suspects for longer periods without charge and the extension of the retirement age, or George W. Bush's folksy efforts to defend the rising American death toll in Iraq or the lamentable efforts of the federal government to deal with the consequences of Hurricane Katrina in New Orleans, rely on insufferable techniques of cultural distortion and dumbing down. Frank Furedi (2004: 72) gets it right when he submits:

> Spoon-feeding the public with sound bites has become a highly prized political skill. Professional speech-writers pursue their task as if their audience was composed of easily distracted children and, not surprisingly, political discussion tends to be shallow, short-termist and bereft of ideas.

Western politicians deplore the apathy and disengagement of the electorate. But the culture of dumbing down that they perpetuate, backed up by the full panoply of instant focus groups and the tough-sounding but specious mechanics of the audit culture, increases levels of cynicism and apathy among the electorate in respect of the organized political process. This raises issues about the meaning of cultural politics in contemporary society.

Contemporary politics appears to be hopelessly trapped in a pincer hold. One side is dominated by the revulsion of the electorate in the face of a political system that is regarded as corrupt and beyond reform. The other side is obsessed with the rise of blatant personality politics, in which image dominates over issues, exemplified by the election of Ronald Reagan to the US Presidency and Arnold Schwarzenegger to the governorship of California, with its grotesque attention-seeking policies of Star Wars, tax cuts and zero tolerance.

Can contemporary representational politics break this pincer hold? Probably not. Active citizenship has made the electorate more informed about the dilemmas and options facing government and society. But one of the unintentional effects that arise from it is the fragmentation of the electorate into a range of interest groups and social movements that vie with each other for state recognition and resource distribution. Strategic unity is possible between these groups, but it is limited by being confined to particular issues, resting on shifting and unreliable alliances, and involves a different kind of cultural politics than prevailed in the past. The question in cultural politics has long since stopped revolving around the national-popular imperative that the lever of state control must eventually pass into the hands of the representatives of the working class. The state must now address multiple interests expressed in the context of real and ideal forms of multicultural society, in which popular ideas of belonging and solidarity are more elusive and ambiguous and in which global forces penetrate more deeply than ever before. The traditional concept of hegemony remains helpful in addressing this state of affairs, but only if it is shorn of its old class connotations. While the means of cultural inclusion can be guaranteed at the level of representational politics by the guarantee of free elections and fixed electoral terms, the scale of popular culture means that some individuals and groups are bound to feel under-represented or misrepresented by the organized political process. If this is the case, governments are likely to be impelled to present policies at the lowest common denominator with a view to maximizing popular support. It follows that large sections of the electorate will feel patronized by this strategy and, further, that levels of apathy and cynicism will be hard to dispel.

As for the presentational issues of representative politics, the probability is that the techniques of image-making developed in celebrity culture will remain pivotal. We still live in Benjamin's culture of the image. Indeed the techniques of marketing images and the public relations systems organized around them have become infinitely more sophisticated in achieving deep consumer penetration. The cultural production of electorally acceptable images of personality is the business of public relations. Typically, PR people use cultural and psychological knowledge to position leaders and figureheads in political culture. Proponents of the thesis of postmodernity or late modernity are right to draw attention to the surface, depthless character of a culture organized around images. Yet in forms of society where types of solidarity are likely to be organized more and more by impersonal connections between people and in which mass communications are central in representation, exchange and contact, the issue is unlikely to dissipate.

So if organized electoral politics is blighted by these problems, should we assume that cultural politics is a dead duck? This takes us back to Marcuse's famous old 1960s nightmare image of 'one dimensional society' (1964), organized around a bureaucratic technocratic power structure, in which genuine political opposition is simply excluded because no realistic alternative prevails. Cultural pessimism is a tempting and understandable response to the situation of hopeless resignation that seems to define many people's attitude to organized politics. But who wants to go there? And isn't pessimism a reactionary response that arises from powerlessness and a lack of engagement with cultural and political life?

Another culture

Earlier I referred to Salman Rushdie's comment, made during the time of the fatwa, that although he disapproved of many aspects of British culture he chose to remain because he felt connected to 'another Britain'.[1] I want to link this observation to Charles Taylor's recent attempt (2004) to revitalize the concept of the imaginary especially with respect to our understanding of culture and society. I think that the imaginary is an ambivalent but indispensable concept for Cultural Studies. In the words of Taylor (2004: 25) it refers to

> that largely unstructured and inarticulate understanding of our whole situation, within which particular features of our world show up for us in the sense they have. It can never be adequately expressed in the form of explicit doctrines because of its unlimited and indefinite nature.

It embraces our shared ways of being together in the world, and the cultural representations through which belonging and protecting a moral order that recognizes mutual benefit are developed and exchanged. The imaginary is influenced by social and cultural theory, but it is always prior and supplemental to it. It is the outcome of popular culture in that it arises from the perceptions, myths, dreams and practices of the people in interplay with active forces of economic, political, technological and social power, regulation and inequality. In common with the idea of 'the public sphere', to which it is related, it is both a real and an ideal space in which ordinary people imagine their surroundings, exploit shared resources and develop mutual 'possibilities'. Like every aspect of culture it is prone to distortion. We imagine ourselves to be free and equal citizens living in a democratic state. But if we make the error of mistaking these cultural principles for *accomplished* cultural conditions we will miss the various ways in which social exclusion, injustice and disempowerment persist and operate in culture. Ideology and false consciousness can certainly be found in the cultural imaginary. But, as Taylor (2004: 183) notes, they are never *just* ideology and false consciousness because they have a 'constitutive function': 'that of making possible the practices that they make sense of and thus enable'.

In an echo of William's phrase 'the long revolution' (1965), Taylor (2004: 185) speaks of 'the long march' of the imaginary. He connects it with deeply rooted struggles of resistance and the construction of traditions of hope organized around the prospect of an enriched social, cultural and economic order. This is a process involving the pattern and cross-cutting of relations of class, race, gender, subculture, locality and nation. Increasingly, the references it draws upon and represents are global and multicultural. At its most forceful and compelling, it mixes a utopian element, in projecting a better general collective future, with a carnivalesque spirit that recognizes the needless limitations and false impasses of the present. The cultural imaginary is where we connect with other ways of being which are not so much repressed or excluded from the present, as popularly felt to exist as latent forces in our lives today. Through the development and exchange of these cultural representations culture expands and is refined.

I think that this is where cultural politics fundamentally operates: in schools, universities, workplaces, pubs, sports arenas, coffee bars, clubs, theatres, on TV, in films, in music and poetry, and in many other cultural settings in which the popular sense of the way things are, the way things go, and how things ought to be are exchanged and developed. Culture is, as Raymond Williams told us, 'ordinary'. This is precisely why it means so much to people, why people argue for its sake and fight wars in its name. It is the warp and woof through which identity, belonging and difference is communicated and internalized.

The imaginary is the 'other culture' to which Rushdie expressed a sense of belonging and kinship when he used the phrase 'another Britain'. With respect to the context of Rushdie's remark, it is coded by national (British) traditions and historical trajectories of development. But the content of aspirations, hopes and dreams in national cultural imaginaries are theoretically all-inclusive. To be sure, the arts, in which the cultural imaginary perhaps achieves its most profound expression, constitute a cultural universal with the capacity to dissolve the many divisions and frictions of religion, race, ethnicity and politics.

Taylor's account of the cultural imaginary fastens upon its role in enriching mutual benefit through articulating and refining the popular meaning of justice, equality, tolerance and liberty. He regards it as harnessing and reinforcing the progressive, democratic impulse in human development. It is opposed to alternative anti-democratic imaginaries that picture 'another culture' in terms of sexual and racial superiority advocated on the grounds of what is often now called an 'invisible intelligence', self-interest and might, prosaically portrayed as right. Taylor's cultural imaginary is presented as enlarging common culture by supporting the cultural ends of social inclusion, distributive justice and empowerment.

A form of Cultural Studies that concerns itself only with means is unlikely to touch these questions because it does not frontally address structures of economic, political, social and cultural scarcity. It tends to focus on making the car go better, rather than asking if we are sitting in the right car or who is left outside. The cultural imaginary is perpetually concerned with cultural ends since it starts from the premise that culture can be *better* as well as different. This is why, for all of its emphasis upon poetry, dreams and other forms of artistic expression, it offers a resource of hard *realism* in advancing cultural politics.

We return to the need for Cultural Studies to be political. The struggle of ordinary people to go beyond the limitations of inequality and scarcity to enhance distributive justice and enlarge social inclusion is the central dynamic of the cultural imaginary. Its *ordinary* nature needs to be prominently stressed. In speculating on the emergence of *world culture*, the American sociologists Frank Lechner and John Boli (2005: 122) highlight the pivotal importance of three players: multinational corporations (Coca-Cola, Sony, Gucci, Burger King); International Government Organizations (IGOs) (the International Monetary Fund, the World Bank, the World Trade Organization, the United Nations, the World Social Forum); and International Nongovernment Organizations (INOs) (voluntary organizations and associations involved in exchanging information and raising consciousness about a plethora of international issues, such as the Rainforest Action Group, Friends of the Earth, the International Social Science Council and the International Red Cross). In evaluating the comparative importance of each player, Lechner and Boli (2005: 121) attribute 'primacy' to INOs. They do so for two reasons.

Firstly, INOs represent virtually every aspect of human endeavour and aspiration. Even if they are partly divided by their specific objectives, they constitute a unifying network in the struggle against inequality, scarcity and widening distributive justice and social and cultural inclusion. Secondly, they are nonprofit organizations which promote common benefits and public goods in the name of common culture. They are concerned to achieve justice rather than with the task of accumulating power. They do so by articulating a system of ethical ends and principles of conduct which are unhampered by pragmatic economic goals or political exigencies. In that sense, they are *disinterested* bodies, who have no shareholders to answer to and seek only to represent the interests of ordinary members and voluntary subscribers.

International Nongovernment Organizations may be thought of as concrete global expressions of the cultural imaginary. They draw on aspirations, hopes, dreams and alternative philosophies that arise from practical engagement with inequality and scarcity, often waged in national locations, but recognize that the ultimate context in which culture is situated is now global. Much can be accomplished at the local and national level, but the supplement to both is the global. This is likely to become historically more pronounced as global forces penetrate more nakedly and deeply into local and national cultures, which, I think, is inevitable in a wired-up world. A political hiatus has developed between International Nongovernment Organizations and International Government Organizations and national governments. It is symbolized by the organized protests that now typically accompany G8 summit meetings and international government conferences and symposia. Organized official political culture now trails an extensive net to counter organizations and critical movements that continuously present different positions and arguments. The rise of active citizenship, the development of global International Nongovernment Organizations and the expansion of the internet have altered the balance between culture and politics by making the active force of the cultural imaginary less marginal or subterranean. Critical discourse, which is the primary medium of the cultural imaginary, is now far more prominent in the public sphere.

The cross-fertilization of the imaginary between races, nations, classes and subcultures offers an exciting range of possibilities for the development of identity and cultural practice. Already a sort of identity 'doublethink' has been proposed in the literature on cultural identity (Hall 1996, 1997). According to it, for the moment we must act, and politically organize, in the name of identity. But through understanding more clearly how representation, theming and coding function, we can already see and *imagine* the disfigurations of closure, distortion and exclusion that are embedded in the concept. Yet we do not possess a language that enables us to combine the mutual liberation that this imagination implies with a cultural politics capable of resisting the forces of imposed cultural genre, distortion, production and consumption. We are in a sort of cultural limbo.

And this is a lesson that doing Cultural Studies regularly teaches and re-teaches as 'the long march' continues but, because of the permanent nature of deconstruction, demystification and demythologization, never ends. Cultural Studies is located between the boundaries of what passes for orthodoxy, and what strains as *possibility* in culture. This is what makes it engrossing and worthwhile. We are constantly engaging with how things go on in the world, what makes them ordinarily acceptable, how they join together, why they fall apart and how they *ought* to be. This engagement with the cultural imaginary often has very concrete policy outcomes. But it is crucial to insist upon the value of its speculative quality, which, of course, is the ultimate value of the imaginary itself. Through dreaming of the not yet born, no less than connecting up with how current political, economic, social and cultural power positions and frequently *stifles* potential, Cultural Studies contributes to illuminating how force and resistance operate in the world, through the relationship of culture to scarcity, inequality and the active material forces of coding, representation and theming. It is why Cultural Studies must ultimately be ranked as a contribution to that best of all human practices: *emancipation*.

Notes

Chapter 4   Zeroing in on Culture

1   The fullest expression of this argument is perhaps the Frankfurt School's 'culture industry thesis' (Adorno and Horkheimer 1944; Marcuse 1964).

Chapter 6   Situating Yourself in Culture

1   The phrase a 'posthumous existence' comes from John Keats in one of his selected letters, written after his fatal illness of tuberculosis was diagnosed.
2   The term 'cultural dope' was coined by the American sociologist Harold Garfinkel.

Chapter 10   Conclusion: The 'Long March' of the Cultural Imaginary

1   Rushdie now divides his time between London and New York.

References

Adorno, T. and Horkheimer, M. (1944). *Dialectic of Enlightenment*. London, Verso.

Ainley, P. (1994). *Degrees of Difference: Higher Education in the 90s*. London, Lawrence & Wishart.

Althusser, L. (1971). *Lenin and Philosophy and Other Essays*. London, New Left Books.

Arnold, M. (1869). *Culture & Anarchy*. Cambridge, Cambridge University Press.

Bahro, R. (1978). *The Alternative in Eastern Europe*. London, Verso.

Bakhtin, M. (1968). *Rabelais and his World*. Cambridge, Mass., MIT Press.

Barthes, R. (1957). *Mythologies*. London, Paladin.

Barthes, R. (1977). *Image-Music-Text*. London, Fontana.

Barthes, R. (1992). *The Grain of the Voice*. Berkeley, University of California Press.

Baudrillard, J. (1983). *Simulations*. New York, Semiotext(e).

Baudrillard, J. (1987). *The Evil Demon of Images*. Sydney, Power Institute.

Baudrillard, J. (1995). *The Gulf War Did Not Take Place*. Bloomington, Indiana University Press.

Beecher, T. and Kogan, M. (1992). *Process and Structure in Higher Education*. London, Routledge.

Benjamin, W. (2003). 'The Work of Art in the Age of its Technological Reproducibility'. In *Selected Writings*, Vol. 4: *1938–40*. Cambridge, Mass. and London, Belknap: 251–83.

Bennett, O. (2001). *Cultural Pessimism*. Edinburgh, Edinburgh University Press.

Bennett, T. (1992). 'Putting Policy into Cultural Studies'. In L. Grossberg, C. Nelson and P. Treichler (eds) *Cultural Studies*. London, Routledge: 23–37.

Bennett, T. (1998). *Culture – A Reformer's Science*. London, Sage.

Billig, M. (1992). *Talking About the Royal Family*. London, Routledge.

Bourdieu, P. (1984). *Distinction*. London, Routledge.

Briffault, R. (1965). *The Troubadours*. Bloomington, Indiana University Press.

Butler, J. (1993). *Bodies That Matter*. London, Routledge.

Butler, J. (1999). *Excitable Speech*. London, Routledge.

Cohen, S. (1972). *Folk Devils and Moral Panics*. London, Paladin.

Corner, J. (2002). 'Performing the Real: Documentary Diversions'. *Television and New Media* 3(3): 255–69.

Couldry, N. (2003). *Media Rituals*. London and New York, Routledge.

Couldry, N. (2004). 'Teaching Us to Fake it: The Ritualized Norms of Television's "Reality" Games'. In S. Murray and L. Ouellette (eds) *Reality TV: Remaking Television Culture*. New York, New York University Press: 57–74.

Coward, R. and Ellis, J. (1977). *Language and Materialism*. London, Routledge and Kegan Paul.

Cressey, P. (1932). *The Taxi Driver Hall*. Chicago, University of Chicago Press.

Culler, J. (1981). *The Pursuit of Signs*. Ithaca, Cornell University Press.

Dale, T. (2005). 'The Contemporary Student Experience and the Transformation of University Life'. Diss., Department of Sociology, University of Portsmouth.

Davis, J. (2003). *Intellectual Property Law*. London, Lexis Nexis.

Department for Culture, Media and Sport (DCMS) (2000). *Centres For Social Change: Museums, Galleries and Archives for All*. London, DCMS.

Derrida, J. (1976). *Of Grammatology*. Baltimore, Johns Hopkins University Press.

Deuber-Mankowsky, A. (2005). *Lara Croft: Cyber Heroine*. Minneapolis, Minnesota University Press.

Dubin, S. (1994). *Arresting Images*. New York, Routledge.

Eco, U. (1976). *A Theory of Semiotics*. Bloomington, Indiana University Press.

Eliot, T.S. (1948). *Notes Towards the Definition of Culture*. London, Faber.

Florida, R. (2002). *The Rise of the Creative Class*. New York, Basic Books.

Foucault, M. (1970). *The Order of Things*. London, Tavistock.

Foucault, M. (1977). *Discipline and Punish*. Harmondsworth, Penguin.

Foucault, M. (1979). *The History of Sexuality*, Vol. 1. Harmondsworth, Penguin.

Frank, T. (1997). *The Conquest of Cool*. Chicago, University of Chicago Press.

Furedi, F. (2004). *Where have all the Intellectuals Gone?* London, Continuum.

Garber, M. (1997). *Vested Interests*. New York, Routledge.

Garnham, N. (1992). 'The Media and the Public Sphere'. In C. Calhoun (ed.) *Habermas and the Public Sphere*. Cambridge, Mass., MIT Press.

Giddens, A. (1994). 'Living in a Post-Traditional Society'. In U. Beck, A. Giddens and C. Lash (eds) *Reflexive Modernization*. Cambridge, Polity.

Gilroy, P. (1987). *There Ain't No Black In The Union Jack*. London, Unwin Hyman.

Gilroy, P. (1993). *The Black Atlantic*. Cambridge, Mass., Harvard University Press.

Goffman, E. (1959). *The Presentation of Self in Everyday Life*. Harmondsworth, Penguin.

Goldburg, J. (1994). *Reclaiming Sodomy*. New York, Routledge.

Goldstein, P. (2003). *Copyright's Highway: From Gutenberg to the Celestial Jukebox*. Stanford, Stanford University Press.

Gramsci, A. (1971). *Selections From Prison Notebooks*. London, Lawrence & Wishart.

Grossberg, L., Nelson, C. and Treichler, P. (1992). *Cultural Studies*. London, Routledge.

Habermas, J. (1962). *The Structural Transformation of the Public Sphere*. Cambridge, Polity.

Hall, S. (1973). 'Encoding and Decoding in the Television Discourse'. Occasional Paper, Birmingham Centre for Contemporary Cultural Studies.

Hall, S. (1979). *Drifting into a Law and Order Society*. London, Cobden Trust.

Hall, S. (1980). 'Cultural Studies: Two Paradigms'. *Media, Culture & Society* 2(2): 57–72.

Hall, S. (1989). 'Authoritarian Populism'. In R. Jessop (ed.) *Thatcherism: A Tale of Two Nations*. Cambridge, Polity: 99–107.

Hall, S. (1992) 'The West and the Rest: Discourses and Power'. In S. Hall and B. Gieben, *Formations of Modernity*. Cambridge, Polity: 275–332.

Hall, S. (1995). 'Fantasy, Identity, Politics'. E. Carter, J. Donald and J. Squires (eds) *Cultural Remix*. London, Lawrence & Wishart: 63–9.

Hall, S. (1996). 'Intoduction: Who Needs Identity?' In P. Dugan and S. Hall (eds) *Questions of Cultural Identity*. London, Sage.

Hall, S. (1997). 'Culture and Power'. *Radical Philosophy* 86: 24–41.

Hall, S., Critcher, C., Jefferson, T., Clarke, J. and Roberts, R. (1978). *Policing the Crisis*. London, Macmillan.

Hall, S., Hobson, D., Lowe, A. and Willis, P. (1980). *Culture, Media, Language*. London, Unwin Hyman.

Hartley, J. (2003). *A Short History of Cultural Studies*. London and Thousand Oaks, Calif., Sage.

Harvey, D. (2005). *The New Imperialism*. Oxford, Oxford University Press.

Hebdige, D. (1979). *Subculture: The Meaning of Style*. London, Routledge.

Hoggart, R. (1958). *The Uses of Literacy*. Harmondsworth, Penguin.

Jameson, F. (1992). *Postmodernism, or The Cultural Logic of Late Capitalism*. Durham, NC, Duke University Press.

Jones, P. (2004). *Raymond Williams's Sociology of Culture*. Basingstoke, Palgrave Macmillan.

Kahney, L. (2004). *The Cult of The Mac*. San Francisco, No Starch Press.

Klein, N. (2001). *No Logo*. London, Flamingo.

Lacan, J. (1970). *Ecrits*. London, Routledge.

Laclau, E. and Mouffe, C. (1985). *Hegemony and Socialist Strategy*. London, Verso.

Leavis, F.R. (1962). *Two Cultures?* London, Chatto & Windus.

Leavis, F.R. (1948). *Education and the University*. London, Chatto & Windus.

Lechner, F. and Boli, J. (2005). *World Culture*. Oxford, Blackwell.

Levine, S. (2004). *The Art of Downloading Music*. London, Sanctuary.

Lévi-Strauss, C. (1962). *The Savage Mind*. Chicago, University of Chicago Press.

Leyda, J. (1988). *Eisenstein on Disney*. London, Methuen.

Linzmayer, O.W. (2004). *Apple Confidential 2.0*. San Francisco, No Starch Press.

Lukacs, G. (1962). *The Theory of the Novel*. London, Merlin.

Lynd, R.S. and Lynd, H.M. (1928). *Middletown*. New York, Harcourt & Brace.

Lyotard, J.F. (1984). *The Postmodern Condition*. Manchester, Manchester University Press.

McGuigan, J. (1992). *Cultural Populism*. London, Routledge.

McGuigan, J. (1996). *Culture and the Public Sphere*. London, Routledge.

McGuigan, J. (2000). 'British Identity and "the people's princess"'. *Sociological Review* 48(1): 1–18.

McGuigan, J. (2004). *Rethinking Cultural Policy*. Maidenhead, Open University Press.

McGuigan, J. (2006). 'The Politics of Cultural Studies and Cool Capitalism'. *Cultural Politics* 2(2).

McRobbie, A. (1978). 'Working Class Girls and the Culture of Femininity'. In Women's Study Group, *Women Take Issue*. London, Hutchinson: 96–108.

McRobbie, A. (1991). *Feminism and Youth Culture*. London, Unwin Hyman.

McRobbie, A. (1996). 'All The World's a Stage, Screen or Magazine'. *Media, Culture & Society* 18(2): 335–42.

Mann, J. (2004). *Rise of the Vulcans*. New York, Penguin.

Mann, M. (2005). *Incoherent Empire*. London, Verso.

Marcuse, H. (1964). *One Dimensional Man*. London, Abacus.

Marx, K. and Engels, F. (1848). 'Manifesto of the Communist Party'. In *Marx/Engels: Selected Works in One Volume*. London, Lawrence and Wishart, 1968.

Mercer, C. (2002). *Towards Cultural Citizenship*. Stockholm, Bank of Sweden Tercentenary Foundation and Gidlungs Forlag.

Meredyth, D. and Minson, J. (eds) (2001). *Citizenship and Cultural Policy*. London, Sage.

Morris, M. (2006). *Identity Anecdotes*. London, Sage.

Naughton, J. (2005). 'File-Sharing Lives on. Honest'. *The Observer* 3.07.05.

Nelson, C. and Grossberg, L. (eds) (1988). *Marxism and the Interpretation of Culture*. Urbana, University of Illinois Press.

Nottingham Trent University Grapevine (2005). 22(1): 13.

Orwell, G. (1940). 'Boys' Weeklies'. <orwell.ru/library.essays/boys/english/e>.

Orwell, G. (1968). *Collected Essays*, Vol. 2. Harmondsworth, Penguin.

Packard, V. (1957). *The Hidden Persuaders*. London, Longman.

Packard, V. (1959). *The Status Seekers*. New York, David Mackay.

Park, T., Burgess, R. and Mackenzie, E. (1925). *The City*. Chicago, University of Chicago Press.

Pieterse, J.N. (2004). *Globalization & Culture*. Boston, Rowman & Littlefield.

Riesman, D. (1950). *The Lonely Crowd*. New York, Doubleday.

Ritzer, G. (1992). *The McDonaldization of Society*. Thousand Oaks, Calif. and London, Pine Forge.

Rojek, C. (2001). *Celebrity*. London, Reaktion.

Rojek, C. (2004). *Frank Sinatra*. Cambridge, Polity.

Rushdie, S. (1988). *The Satanic Verses*. London, Jonathan Cape.

Said, E. (1978). *Orientalism*. Harmondsworth, Penguin.

Said, E. (1993). *Culture and Imperialism*. New York, Vintage; London, Chatto & Windus.

Saussure, F. de (1915). *Course in General Linguistics*. New York, McGraw Hill.

Schuller, T. (ed.) (1991). *The Changing University?* Buckingham, SRHE and Open University Press.

Scott, P. (1995). *The Meanings of Mass Higher Education.* Buckingham, SRHE & Open University Press.

Sturrock, J. (ed.) (1979). *Structuralism and Since.* Oxford, Oxford University Press.

Taylor, C. (2004). *Modern Social Imaginaries.* Durham, NC, Duke University Press.

Theweleit, K. (1989). *Male Fantasies*, Vol. 2. Cambridge, Polity.

Thomas, W. and Zaniecki, F. (1929). *The Polish Peasant in Europe and America.* Chicago, University of Chicago Press.

Thompson, E.P. (1963). *The Making of the English Working Class.* Harmondsworth, Penguin.

Turner, G. (1990). *British Cultural Studies.* London, Unwin Hyman.

Tylor, E.B. (1874). *Primitive Culture.* Boston, Estes and Lauriat.

Volosinov, V.N. (1973). *Marxism and the Philosophy of Language.* New York, Seminar Press.

West, C. (1992). 'The Postmodern Crisis of the Black Intellectuals'. In L. Grossberg, C. Nelson and P. Treichler (eds) *Cultural Studies.* London, Routledge.

Whyte, W. (1943). *Street Corner Society.* Chicago, University of Chicago Press.

Williams, J. (1998). 'Editorial Instinct: An Interview with William P. Germano'. *The Minnesota Review* (the minnesotareview.org/ns48/germano.htm 48–9): 1–13.

Williams, R. (1958). 'Culture is Ordinary'. In N. McKenzie (ed.). *Conviction.* London, MacGibbon & Kee.

Williams, R. (1963). *Culture and Society 1780–1950.* Harmondsworth, Penguin.

Williams, R. (1965). *The Long Revolution.* Harmondsworth, Penguin.

Willis, P. (1977). *Learning to Labour.* Farnborough, Saxon House.

Women's Studies Group (WSG) (1978). *Women Take Issue.* London, Hutchinson.

Žižek, S. (1997). *The Plague of Fantasies.* London, Verso.

Zorbaugh, H.W. (1929). *The Gold Coast and the Slum.* Chicago, University of Chicago Press.

Author Index

Subject Index